To Reverend Williams Blanks
May God bless you—

This series offers the concerned reader basic guidelines and *practical* applications of religion for today's world. Although decidedly Christian in focus and emphasis, the series embraces all denominations and modes of Bible-based belief relevant to our lives today. All volumes in the Steeple series are originals, freshly written to provide a fresh perspective on current—and yet timeless—human dilemmas. This is a series for our times. Among the books:

Woman in Despair:
A Christian Guide to Self-Repair
Elizabeth Rice Handford

A Spiritual Handbook for Women
Dandi Daley Knorr

How to Read the Bible
James Fischer

Bible Solutions
to Problems of Daily Living
James W. Steele

A Book of Devotions
for Today's Woman
Frances Carroll

Temptation:
How Christians Can Deal with It
Frances Carroll

With God on Your Side:
A Guide to Finding Self-Worth
Through Total Faith
Doug Manning

Help in Ages Past, Hope for Years
to Come: Daily Devotions
from the Old Testament
Robert L. Cate

A Daily Key for Today's Christians:
365 Key Texts of the New Testament
William E. Bowles

Walking in the Garden:
Inner Peace from the Flowers of God
Paula Connor

How to Bring up Children
in the Catholic Faith
Carol and David Powell

Sex in the Bible:
An Introduction to
What the Scriptures
Teach Us About Sexuality
Michael R. Cosby

How to Talk with God
Every Day of the Year:
A Book of Devotions
for Twelve Positive Months
Frances Hunter

God's Conditions for Prosperity:
How to Earn the Rewards
of Christian Living
Charles Hunter

Pilgrimages: A Guide to
the Holy Places of Europe
for Today's Traveler
Paul Lambourne Higgins

Journey into the Light:
Lessons of Pain and Joy to Renew
Your Energy and Strengthen Your Faith
Dorris Blough Murdock

Frances Hunter, the author of more than twenty books, is actively involved with her husband, Charles, in a dynamic worldwide ministry of evangelism through teaching, books, radio, television, magazine articles, a publishing company, and a Bible school. She and her husband are co-directors of the City of Light Christian Center in Texas.

Prentice-Hall International, Inc., *London*
Prentice Hall of Australia Pty. Limited, *Sydney*
Prentice-Hall Canada Inc., *Toronto*
Prentice-Hall of India Private Limited, *New Delhi*
Prentice-Hall of Japan, Inc., *Tokyo*
Prentice-Hall of Southeast Asia Pte. Ltd., *Singapore*
Whitehall Books Limited, *Wellington, New Zealand*
Editora Prentice-Hall do Brasil Ltda., *Rio de Janeiro*

Frances Hunter

HOW TO TALK WITH GOD EVERY DAY OF THE YEAR

A Book of Devotions for Twelve Positive Months

Prentice-Hall, Inc., Englewood Cliffs, New Jersey 07632

Library of Congress Cataloging in Publication Data

Hunter, Frances Gardner (date).
How to talk with God every day of the year.

(Steeple books)
Rev. ed. of: A confession a day keeps the devil away! /
by Charles and Frances Hunter. c1980.
"A Spectrum Book."
1. Devotional calendars. I. Hunter, Charles
(date). Confession a day keeps the devil away!
II. Title. III. Series.
BV4811.H86 1983 242'.2 83-13855
ISBN 0-13-435248-3
ISBN 0-13-435230-0 (pbk.)

A Spectrum Book. Printed in the United States of America.

Previously published as *A Confession a Day Keeps the Devil Away!*
by Hunter Books, Humble, Texas. © 1980 by Charles and Frances Hunter.

ISBN 0-13-435248-3

ISBN 0-13-435230-0 {PBK.}

10 9 8 7 6 5 4 3 2 1

Editorial/production supervision by Betsy Torjussen
Cover design by Hal Siegel
Manufacturing buyer: Edward J. Ellis

This book is available at a special discount when ordered in
bulk quantities. Contact Prentice-Hall, Inc., General
Publishing Division, Special Sales, Englewood Cliffs, N.J. 07632.

Contents

Grateful acknowledgment is given to the following for granting permission to reprint passages from their publications:

HOW TO TALK WITH GOD EVERY DAY OF THE YEAR

Introduction

Let's talk to God every day of the year. He'll listen. Prayer connects us to a direct hot line to heaven that has never returned a busy signal to any caller. Prayer is simply talking with God. It has many forms and many degrees of intensity: Sometimes it's an urgent need; sometimes it's a down-the-road request. Whatever it is, there's an answer!

Paul tells us in I Thessalonians 5:17 to *pray without ceasing*. The Living Bible tells us to *Always keep on praying*. The Amplified Bible says to *Be unceasing in prayer—praying perseveringly.* From this we should get the message that our conversational line to God should be kept open at all times.

Lack of communication can be a problem, whether it's between a wife and husband, parents and children, employer and employees, or brothers and sisters. Communication lines can become clogged when they're not used often enough. They can become overloaded with filth and lies when we don't keep routing them out with truth. *Even the communication lines with God can become encumbered with doubt and unbelief unless we keep them in constant use.*

Anything that is not used atrophies or disintegrates from not being used. Did you ever see a beautiful house that was left vacant? Before long, the house looks run down and doesn't even resemble the original structure.

Did you ever put a dress to one side of your closet because it was "too good" to wear all the time? Did you notice when you took it out again that it didn't look quite as lovely as you had expected it to look? Just letting it hang in the closet did something to it that is hard to explain.

So it is with prayer. God tells us to *Ask, and it shall be given you; seek, and ye shall find; knock, and it shall be opened unto you* (Matthew 7:7). He's never too busy, never too tired, never too disinterested to hear us when we call.

He promises to answer. That is why it is so important that we know what promises the Bible contains, so we can receive all the good things that God has for us. Think about what God promises to give us in the following Scriptures: *He shall call upon me, and I will answer him: I will be with him in trouble; I will deliver him, and honour him* (Psalm 91:15). What a promise! He promises to be with us when we call—he'll never be away from that telephone—and he promises to answer us. What is so precious about this Scripture is that he says beyond a shadow of a doubt that he will definitely answer us. That heartfelt cry to God in prayer when you are in trouble has a built-in guarantee that he will deliver you!

In Isaiah 58:9 the Lord says, *Then shalt thou call, and the Lord shall answer; thou shalt cry, and he shall say, Here I am. If thou take away from the midst of thee the yoke, the putting forth of the finger, and speaking vanity.* What God is really saying is that if you will take every burden from others, giving instead of wanting to receive everything for yourself; if you will stop pointing an accusing finger at someone else and quit all boasting and being full of pride, he'll say, "Here I am!" God himself is the answer to your prayer.

I love the promptness of God—in Isaiah 65:24 he says, *And it shall come to pass, that before they call, I will answer; and while they are yet speaking, I will hear.* What an encouragement to pray, knowing that he will answer your prayer even before you pray.

Another guarantee of his promptness is found in Jeremiah 33:3 when he says, *Call unto me, and I will answer thee, and shew thee great and mighty things, which thou knowest not.* He promises to show us answers through great and mighty things that we don't even know about yet.

In John 15:7 it says, *If you abide in me, and my words abide in you, ye shall ask what ye will, and it shall be done unto you. Abide* means to "go into," so if we "go into" God, and his words go into us, then we can ask and it is definitely going to be done for us!

With all these positive things going for us, we ought to spend more time communicating with God and putting our needs and wants before him.

> Put this book where you can see it and speak some of these prayers several times every day and see what happens to you. Read each day's prayer to God several times during the day until the Word of God "sticks to your ribs," or gets into your heart! When you read the prayer for the day, read it out loud so you can hear it—*So then faith cometh by hearing, and hearing by the word of God* (Romans 10:17).

Get your family together and read the devotion for the day together. There's power in agreement, so when an entire family agrees on the prayer for the day, there is a tremendous bombardment at the gates of heaven for your needs.

It's an extra blessing to see family unity strengthened by reading and praying God's Word together. Fussing, complaining, and arguing turn to praising and loving God and one another.

God tells us to put him in remembrance of his Word; so when we pray, we need to pray God's Word, so that we will know that nothing will hinder our prayers.

When we pray God's Word, we are using our tongues to agree with God, and our tongue can make or break us! We can use our tongue to gossip, backbite, criticize, complain, and speak evil reports, or that same tongue can be brought under control and bring praises to God. The same little part of our body can bring happiness or sorrow, depending on what we pray with it. We have both life and death in the power of the tongue, and we can choose which we speak. *Death and life are in the power of the tongue: and they that love it shall eat the fruit thereof* (Proverbs 18:21). So let's remember to *let the Words of my mouth . . . be acceptable in thy sight, O Lord* (Psalm 19:14).

You Can Have What You Say When You Pray!

For verily I say unto you, That whosoever shall say unto this mountain, Be thou removed, and be thou cast into the sea; and shall not doubt in his heart, but shall believe that those things which he saith shall come to pass; he shall have whatsoever he saith (Mark 11:23).

There is so much to be said about that Scripture that ten thousand sermons could be preached on it and an equal number of books could be written about it.

When we pray, we need to pray "positive" prayers. "Negative" prayers can create problems, because we can speak negative words with such belief that we get exactly what we say and pray.

We have discovered in our prayer life that it is far better to pray the Word of God rather than the problem. Instead of praying, "Oh God, I'll never have enough money to pay my bills," start praying, "Thank you, Father, that your Word says that you will supply all my needs according to your riches in glory through Christ Jesus!"

When we speak with our own lips about sickness and disease, we are speaking exactly what the devil wants us to say; but when we pray God's Word about healing and deliverance, we call into being those things which be not as though they were.

Where do you start, and where do you end? We've chosen different subjects to pray about each month—The Word; Faith; Prosperity; The Name of Jesus; Blessings; Love; Freedom from Fear; Joy; Healing; Holy Spirit; Praise; and Salvation.

What do you do when you need to pray for prosperity and it's January? Jump over into March, where we pray all prosperity prayers, and don't worry about getting out of date or out of order. However, by focusing on one topic each month, you can gain new insights and a new perspective—in short, this method can help you *grow* in your prayer life and as a person.

One of the most important things we have discovered in receiving answers to prayer is to "believe without a doubt." God's Word is true, so if we pray the Word instead of the circumstances, it will be easy for us to believe with absolutely no doubt in our hearts.

Don't get impatient with God. He knows the right timing for the answer to your prayer, and he's never been known to be a single day late! Sometimes in our desire to speed things up we give up just as God starts to answer our prayers, and we lose out. Keep thanking him after you have prayed, keep believing, and NEVER GIVE UP! God doesn't want us to quit—he wants us to be persistent!

God is not a man, that he should lie; neither the son of man, that he should repent: hath he said, and shall he not do it? or hath he spoken, and shall he not make it good? (Numbers 23:19). God cannot lie, or he would be going back on his own Word, so keep believing and know that it will come to pass.

Prayer is not a one-way street. When you pray, listen to God. Too many times we get so busy complaining to God that we forget to open our ears to and shut our mouths so that we can hear God! Remember, he likes to talk too, and the one he wants to talk to is *You*. So wait for an answer!

Maybe praying the answer is something new and different for you, but try it—it works!

January

THE WORD

In the beginning God created the heaven and the earth (Genesis 1:1).

Mr. Webster says that the word *create* means "To originate; to bring into being from nothing; to cause to exist."

God took nothing and from nothing He created the universe.

How did He create it? From Hebrew 11:3 we get the important clue that can unlock the entire Bible for us in a totally new and different way: *Through faith we understand that the worlds were framed by the Word of God, so that things which are seen were not made of things which do appear.*

By the *Word* of God.

Not by the hands of God.

Not by the feet of God.

Not by the mind of God.

Not by the power of God, but

By the Word of God.

We can create a whole new world for ourselves by confessing the Word of God for our lives.

It's one thing to read the Word of God, it's another thing to memorize the Word of God, but when you confess it, what you're saying is *it's mine, it's mine, it's mine!* I take it for myself.

January 1

For the word of God is quick, and powerful, and sharper than any twoedged sword, piercing even to the dividing asunder of soul and spirit, and of the joints and marrow, and is a discerner of the thoughts and intents of the heart (Hebrews 4:12).

Glory, Father, nothing can withstand the sword of your Word, which is mightier and more forceful than all the nuclear power in this world. With that sword in my hand each and every day, there's nothing I can't overcome. I'm a winner, not a loser, because your Word has made it so. I delight and revel in the power of your wonderful Word, which cleanses my heart, lifts my thoughts heavenward, and is like an invincible two-edged sword preparing the way before me. It's quick, too, because it doesn't take long to hit the target.

January 2

For who hath known the mind of the Lord, that he may instruct him? But we have the mind of Christ (I Corinthians 2:16).

Father, what a privilege to know that I'm not operating with a natural mind. I praise You that my thoughts are heavenly because I have the mind of Christ. I thank you that I don't have to worry about those silly things that come into my mind every once in a while. When they start, I can just relax and realize that I have the mind of Christ. I don't have to hang onto the garbage and worries of the world. Instead, I'm concentrating on my eternal destination, and I thank and praise you for that.

January 3

So shall my word be that goeth forth out of my mouth: it shall not return unto me void, but it shall accomplish that which I please, and it shall prosper in the thing whereto I sent it (Isaiah 55:11).

Father, I thank you that your Word does everything that you say it will do. I thank you that it accomplishes exactly what you say, without any "if's," "and's," or "but's." I thank you for the knowledge that nothing your Word says shall ever fall by the wayside and die. I praise you because you've said it never returns to you void. I bless you, Father, that your Word grows, multiplies, thrives, flourishes, blossoms, and blooms wherever and whenever you send it. I praise you that it never dies on the vine, but is constantly growing and multiplying.

January 4

Blessed are they that hear the word of God, and keep it (Luke 11:28).

Father, I bless you because I am blessed. I have heard your Word, and I keep it hidden in my heart, so that I might not sin against you. I thank you that because I keep your Word, I am blessed in everything I do. I thank you because I have had the opportunity to hear your Word. Father, I am blessed among all the people of every nation in the world because I have the opportunity at all times to hear your Word. I thank you for a Word that permeates my entire being and blesses me as I read it, memorize it, and confess it. Father, I am keeping it in my heart forever, and I love you for giving me your Word.

January 5

All scripture is given by inspiration of God, and is profitable for doctrine, for reproof, for correction, for instruction in righteousness (II Timothy 3:16).

Father, I praise you that there is no guesswork with Scripture. I thank you for the knowledge that every single word has been given by inspiration of God. I thank you that you had many purposes in inspiring those men of old to write down your thoughts, because they established doctrine, creed, and dogma for us. I praise you, Father, that your Word has power to rebuke, admonish, and censure us. I bless you that, when I get out of line, your Word is right there to correct me and get me straightened out again. But most of all, Father, I bless you for giving me instructions on how to live in the beauty of your righteousness. Glory, I'm walking in righteousness.

January 6

Heaven and earth shall pass away: but my words shall not pass away (Mark 13:31).

Father, how I praise you because the things of this world are transient—friends are transient, possessions are subject to change, but your Word is not. I bless you that, even though everything else goes down the drain, your words shall remain forever and ever. Thank you, Father, that we come into this world in a perishable container, which we know won't last forever, but you have given us something to put into that temporary housing that will last eternally, and that is your Word. Bless you, Father, that, even when the storms of life are thundering all around us and it looks as though everything may fall apart, I can stand on the secure knowledge that your words shall never pass away.

January 7

And Jesus answered him, saying, It is written, That man shall not live by bread alone, but by every word of God (Luke 4:4).

I praise you, Father, for the spiritual banquet you've given me in your Word. I feast every day on manna, and this body of mine thrives on the heavenly vitamins you provide. I thank you that I do not have to live by the physical things alone, but that I can find spiritual health in your Word, which assures me of a healthy body, a sound mind, and an endless supply of enthusiasm for tackling the tasks you put before me. Father, thank you for not wasting one single word but for making each and every word count in my life. I love you for that.

January 8

If ye abide in me, and my words abide in you, ye shall ask what ye will, and it shall be done unto you (John 15:7).

Father, I love that word *abide*. I praise you that as long as I dwell, reside, live, stay in, and submit to you, and let your words snuggle down deep inside me, you give me the awesome privilege of asking whatever I will and then of resting safe and secure in the knowledge that it will be done for me. I bless you, because you simply gave me these two little conditions—that I have to abide in you, and let your words abide in me—for those blessings of Abraham to overtake and overcome me. Bless you, Father, for not being a stingy God and promising us only one thing for abiding in you, but for promising us everything.

January 9

I will hasten my word to perform it (Jeremiah 1:12).

Father, I bless you that you lose no time performing your Word. I can see you in my mind speeding up and expediting all the things you've promised, because you are not a God who sits back and does nothing, but you are a God of action. I thank you that you make short work of those things that stand in the way of the performance of your Word. I thank you, Father, that you don't use delaying tactics like the devil does, but that you are prompt and right on schedule at all times in fulfilling your Word.

January 10

Thy word have I hid in mine heart, that I might not sin against thee. . . . For ever, O Lord, thy word is settled in heaven (Psalm 119:11, 89).

Father, thank you for letting me hide your wonderful, brilliant, resplendent, dazzling, glorious words in my heart for the purpose of having them there to remind me not to sin. Your words are so sharp and penetrating, they can go through the greatest temptation that might ever come my way to protect me from the fiery darts of the devil himself. I praise you for that weapon with which I can protect myself at all times from sin. And how I thank you, Father, that we have no arguing and debating about your Word, because it has been settled in heaven for all time! Not down here on earth, Father, but right up in heaven with you. Bless you, Father, that I live by heaven-made rules and don't have to depend on the peculiarities of men.

January 11

Thy word is a lamp unto my feet, and a light unto my path (Psalm 119:105).

Father, I bless you that I'm not stumbling around in the dark wondering which way to go. Bless you that you have put your Word as a lamp at my feet, so that I may receive understanding and enlightenment to my mind, my heart, and my soul. Father, I love your law, and I meditate in it day and night because of the glorious light it sheds abroad. I thank you that the path on which I walk is one where I have no fear that I might fall down in the darkness, because it is flooded with light with no hiding places for sin to lurk and get me. Thank you that your light is brighter than any light man has ever developed and that it's turned right onto my path.

January 12

The entrance of thy words giveth light; it giveth understanding unto the simple (Psalm 119:130).

Father, how I thank you that your Word broke through the cold, stony heart I once had. I praise you that when one single word sneaked through that crevice in my sinful armor, it began to give light to my life. Thank you that the unfolding of your Word gave me understanding, discernment, and comprehension, even though my mind was simple. How I longed for your words to give me more and more light, and because of this you were merciful to me, showed me your favor, and established my steps, and directed them by means of your Word. I love your Word, so I will keep on hearing, receiving, loving, and obeying it!

January 13

The law of thy mouth is better unto me than thousands of gold and silver (Psalm 119:72).

Father, how I bless you that the world can have its silver and gold, with its fluctuating prices, but your Word stands above all the treasures of this world and never changes. I praise you because your promises surpass anything this world has to offer. Thank you that your Word is better than silver and gold, houses and lands, or any other kind of material possessions. I thank you that the entrance of your Word illumines my entire life and that you teach me good judgment, wise and right discernment, and knowledge, and that the earth is full of your loving kindness and mercy.

January 14

Therefore whosoever heareth these sayings of mine, and doeth them, I will liken him unto a wise man, which built his house upon a rock: And the rain descended, and the floods came, and the winds blew, and beat upon that house; and it fell not: for it was founded upon a rock (Matthew 7:24).

Father, I praise you that my house is built upon a rock because I have heard your Word and am a doer of the Word, not just a hearer. I bless you that because of this you have called me a wise and productive person, practical in all ways. I bless you, Father, for the promise of your Word that says when the rains fall and the floods overflow, and even when the winds become hurricane force and beat upon my house, it won't fall because it is founded on a rock. Father, I bless you that your Word doesn't allow me to be foolish and build my house upon the sand, so that the winds could blow my house down. I praise you that my house is standing on a solid rock—your Word.

January 15

It is the spirit that quickeneth; the flesh profiteth nothing: the words that I speak unto you, they are spirit, and they are life (John 6:63).

Father, I praise you that the Spirit quickens your Word. I thank you that the Spirit is the Life-giver; there is no profit in the flesh. I thank you that the words which you have spoken and recorded in your Word give me spirit and life. I bless you, Father, that I am not dead in the trespasses of sin and disaster but that I am alive, because my spirit has been quickened, energized, and made alive by your Word.

January 16

Ye are of God, little children, and have overcome them: because greater is he that is in you, than he that is in the world (I John 4:4).

Father, how I applaud and glorify your Word. I thank you for the magnificent promises in your Word. I thank you, Father, that your Son, Jesus Christ, lives big in me; he is greater and mightier than the devil and all his doings. I don't have to submit to the devil's torment any longer, because I know that your Word is true. You have said that there is a greater one living in me than is living in the world, and I believe it, receive it, confess it, and possess this promise for myself. I thank you that, regardless of how big the devil might look to me in certain situations, I can stand tall and look down on him, knowing that I have far more power than he does.

January 17

This book of the law shall not depart out of thy mouth; but thou shalt meditate therein day and night, that thou mayest observe to do according to all that is written therein: for then thou shalt make thy way prosperous, and then thou shalt have good success (Joshua 1:8).

Your Word is in my mouth, Father, and I'm not taking it out. For too many years I spoke the filth of the devil, and I like what you've given me better. I praise you that I am made righteous and have right standing with you because of your saving grace. I thank you that, because I am doing everything according to what is written in your law, I am prospering and having good success. I praise you, Father, that I don't have to depend on the world for instructions on how to be successful, but that I can depend on your Word; you don't make provision for failure, you only make provision for success! I'm prospering, I'm successful, I'm blessed—because *you* said so!

January 18

There is therefore now no condemnation to them which are in Christ Jesus, who walk not after the flesh, but after the Spirit (Romans 8:1).

Father, I thank you that I walk in victory today and *every* day, because I have been redeemed by the blood of the Lamb. I'm washed clean inside out, because the best detergent in the whole world is that precious blood. Therefore, I have no condemnation or guilt in my life, because my sins are washed away *forever.* Father, I'm not interested in walking after the flesh, because that leads to death, but I'm walking after the law of the Spirit of life, which is the law of my new being. It has freed me from the law of sin and death. Hallelujah! I'm not only walking, but I'm dancing in the newness of life.

January 19

What shall we then say to these things? If God be for us, who can be against us? (Romans 8:31).

There's another one of your wonderful promises, Father, and I praise and glorify you, because *you are for me.* Together, you and I make a majority, and nothing and no one can stand against us. Father, by myself I might not be so super, but with you I'm a majority at all times. I bless you that I don't have to rely on my own strength, but I'm walking in your power and might. Together we can move mountains. Hallelujah! I'm victorious because you're on my side. The devil can't win against me, his angels can't win against me, so there is no way they can successfully be against me. You could make it without me, but I sure can't make it without you.

January 20

Therefore if any man be in Christ, he is a new creature: old things are passed away; behold, all things are become new (II Corinthians 5:17).

Father, I praise you that I am in Christ, because I have been born again of the incorruptible seed that can't be contaminated, spoiled, or tainted. I thank you that I am a *new* creature. I praise you that the individual who was me a few short years ago no longer exists. I praise you that all the things of my old nature have passed away and that I'm a brand-new creature in Christ. I praise you that everything about me has changed and that all things are new. I praise you that the month of January always ushers in a new year, and it reminds me of the newness of life in Christ Jesus. I praise you for making me and keeping me new!

January 21

Lie not one to another, seeing that ye have put off the old man with his deeds; And have put on the new man, which is renewed in knowledge after the image of him that created him (Colossians 3:9, 10).

Glory to God, I'm a *new person.* Father, I praise you for making the Christian life so simple, because you so beautifully tell us what to do and what not to do. Thank you that I have put off the old person with all my evil and have put on the new one. I like the new "me" better. I thank you that my mind is renewed and is no longer conformed to this world, because I have been created in your beautiful image. I love you, Father, and praise you for loving me so much that you put all these beautiful promises in your Word.

January 22

Behold, the days come, saith the Lord, when I will make a new covenant with the house of Israel and with the house of Judah. . . . For this is the covenant that I will make with the house of Israel after those days, saith the Lord; I will put my laws into their mind, and write them in their hearts: and I will be to them a God, and they shall be to me a people (Hebrews 8:8, 10).

Father, I praise you and thank you for the new covenant you have given to us. I praise you that I cannot claim ignorance of your covenant, because you have written and imprinted your laws upon my innermost thoughts and understanding and because you have forever engraved them in my heart. I praise you for the way you have inscribed all these laws permanently upon my heart, so that wherever I go, I can never get away from you. Hallelujah! I'm a covenant person.

January 23

And now I beseech thee, lady, not as though I wrote a new commandment unto thee, but that which we had from the beginning, that we love one another. And this is love, that we walk after his commandments. This is the commandment, That, as ye have heard from the beginning, ye should walk in it (II John 5).

Father, how I praise you that you instruct us to live the love life and walk the love life. I'm going to walk and talk the love life at all times and love the unlovely. I praise you for the power you give me to walk this love walk and for the instructions you give me. Father, let this year be the most loving of my life. I praise you for giving me a special infilling of your precious love.

January 24

He that hath an ear, let him hear what the Spirit saith unto the churches; to him that overcometh will I give to eat of the hidden manna, and will give him a white stone, and in the stone a new name written, which no man knoweth saving he that receiveth it (Revelation 2:17).

Father, I praise you for my ears that hear the Spirit. I thank you for letting me be an overcomer in all things through Christ, who strengthens me. I praise you that some day soon I will eat of the hidden manna and will have a brand-new name written in the stone, a name which is just for me. Father, I praise you for your goodness to me. I love you because I don't have to look at the things that are temporal and subject to change, but I look at the things that are eternal and lasting. Hallelujah! My ears are hearing, and I'm overcoming.

January 25

And he that sat upon the throne said, Behold I make all things new. And he said unto me, Write: for these words are true and faithful. And he said unto me, It is done. I am Alpha and Omega, the beginning and the end. I will give unto him that is athirst of the fountain of the water of life freely. He that overcometh shall inherit all things; and I will be his God, and he shall be my son (Revelation 21:5–7).

Jesus, you are the beginning and the end. Your words are true and faithful. You make all things, including me, brand new. I praise you lavishly, because when I was thirsty you gave to me of the water of life freely. I thank you that, because of the power of the Holy Spirit, I am an overcomer at all times. Because of this I shall inherit all things. God, you are my God. Jesus, your redemptive work at Calvary made me God's child. Hallelujah!

January 26

Knowing this, that our old man is crucified with him, that the body of sin might be destroyed, that henceforth we should not serve sin. For he that is dead is freed from sin (Romans 6:6, 7).

Father, how I bless you that with this new year because of my new life, my old man is crucified, lifeless, and inanimate, and I don't have to walk under sin's power and dominion any longer. I praise you that the old, unregenerated, unrenewed man is *dead, dead, dead.* Therefore, I don't have to serve sin any more. Sin is no longer my master. I praise you that when I learned to die to self, you freed me from sin, wickedness, impurity, iniquity, and error. I am now a servant to a new Master, who has revitalized me in the newness of Christ.

January 27

Jesus answered, Verily, verily, I say unto thee, Except a man be born of water and of the Spirit, he cannot enter into the kingdom of God. That which is born of flesh is flesh; and that which is born of the Spirit is spirit (John 3:5, 6).

Father, I praise you that I am living in the *newness* of life because I have been born again by your precious Spirit. I thank you that I am no longer a fleshly creature, subject to the things of this world. Because I have been born again, I am a spiritual being under your control. I praise you that you provided such a beautiful and simple way for me to have eternal life. I'm walking toward the Kingdom of God with a new lilt in my walk, because I'm a *new creation.*

January 28

Be not conformed to this world: but be ye transformed by the renewing of your mind, that ye may prove what is that good, and acceptable, and perfect, will of God (Romans 12:2).

Father, I bless you that in my new life I do not have to be conformed to this world. I don't have to dress the way they do, I don't have to act the way the world acts, and I don't have to talk the way the world does. I praise you that my new life gives me freedom to live the way you want. I thank you that my mind is renewed with new ideas, ideals, and attitudes. I bless you for this. I thank you, Father, that I have presented my body and all its members to you as a living sacrifice, because it is my reasonable and intelligent service to you. I praise you and thank you for your grace that made this all possible. Father, I shall glory in you forever. How perfect are your ways—they are faultless, spotless, and unblemished.

January 29

Being confident of this very thing, that he which hath begun a good work in you will perform it until the day of Jesus Christ (Philippians 1:6).

Father, I praise you for confidence in my *new* life. I bless you that, even though I can't always see the end and perfection of what you have planned for me, I have the complete knowledge and faith that you will keep working in me until the day of Jesus Christ. I praise you, Father, that I don't have to worry, because you have promised to help me in your Word. I praise you because you're still working in me. Because of this, I'm an overcomer, confident that whatever is born of you overcomes the whole world. So I'm going to shout it from the housetops. *I'm an overcomer, I'm an overcomer,* because God is working in me.

January 30

And you are standing there before him with nothing left against you—nothing left that he could even chide you for; the only condition is that you fully believe the Truth, standing in it steadfast and firm, strong in the Lord, convinced of the Good News that Jesus died for you, and never shifting from trusting him to save you (Colossians 1:22, 23 LB).

Father, how I praise you that this new creature stands before you with nothing left for you to chide me for, because you have buried my sins in the deepest sea, never to be remembered again. How I praise you for this. You said the only condition was that I fully believe the truth and stand in it firmly. Father, *I do, I do, I do.* I'm standing tall and straight and can look the world straight in the eye, because my sins are gone, gone, *gone.*

January 31

And we know that all things work together for good to them that love God, to them who are called according to his purpose (Romans 8:28).

Glory, Father, for the fact that everything, everything, *everything* that happens to me works together for my own good. I thank you that you can take the biggest mess and turn everything in it around, so that it turns out for my good. I bless you, Father, that, regardless of how dark and gloomy things look, I know beyond a shadow of doubt that it's working for my good. I praise you that when I call for help the very tide of the battle turns and my enemies flee, all because of you. Thank you that you take any old mess and make a miracle out of it. Thank you, Father, for a month of total victory, because I have stood on your promises. Thank you for the extra prosperity that has come into my house; thank you for the health you have given me; thank you for showing me that miracles and wonders still happen these days; thank you for the marvelous victory you have given me simply by confessing your promises.

February

FAITH

The Christian life is so simple because we only have to do two things:

1. Do what God tells us to do.
2. Stop doing what he tells us not to do!

That's all there is to it, and if you do them, you've got it made!

And how do we do what God wants us to do? The Psalmist tells us, *Thy word have I hid in mine heart, that I might not sin against thee* (119:11) because *For ever, O Lord, thy word is settled in heaven* (119:89).

Once you establish in your own mind that every single word that is printed on the pages of the Bible is the actual spoken Word of God and written down for posterity, your faith can begin that upward climb as you read the Word, confess it, memorize it, and hide it in your heart.

How do you increase your faith? *Faith cometh by hearing, and hearing by the word of God* (Romans 10:17). We need to *hear* the Word of God.

How can we hear the Word of God? By reading the Bible.

The Bible is God's personal love letter to you, and if you will just read it seeking God, believe it, confess it, and live it, then every promise in the Word is yours!

February 1

Now faith is the substance of things hoped for, the evidence of things not seen (Hebrews 11:1).

Thank you, Father, that faith is the pledge and the confirmation of the things we long and hope for, but which we can't see at the moment. We bless you because, even though we do not see some things with our natural eyes, in our spirit we can see them as a reality. Because of this, we can see what is not revealed to our senses. Father, I thank you for Noah, who had never heard of rain, and because he was prompted by faith, he diligently constructed and prepared an ark through the eyes of faith. I thank you that in the twentieth century I can also look with my eyes of faith and see things come to pass that were just a hope in the past. Hallelujah!

February 2

But without faith it is impossible to please him: for he that cometh to God must believe that he is, and that he is a rewarder of them that diligently seek him (Hebrews 11:6).

Father, thank you for making it so plain that, if I don't use the faith you've given me, there is no way I can please you. I bless you, Father, that I don't have to work up something on my own, because your faith is a gift. I believe in you, and I believe that you are the God of all gods. I thank you that you expect me to believe that you are a rewarder of them that diligently seek you. I am and will continue to diligently seek you, and I thank you for rewarding my faith. I bless you that you've made your promises so easy for me to accept through faith. I'm receiving those rewards *right now.*

February 3

Above all, taking the shield of faith, where with ye shall be able to quench all the fiery darts of the wicked (Ephesians 6:16).

Thank you, Father, for surrounding me with your shield of faith, so that I am completely protected from every kind of wickedness. Any kind of wicked temptation, remark, insult, accusation, or attack is quenched and conquered by the shield of faith that I wear constantly. Not even the devil himself can get through it! I walk in the world, and I am not afraid. Nothing can harm me. I walk in faith. I talk in faith. I pray in faith. I rejoice in faith. Father, you are my strength and my fortress, and I praise you, because with my shield of faith I live in victory every minute of the day, every day of the year.

February 4

For I say, through the grace given unto me, to every man that is among you, not to think of himself more highly than he ought to think; but to think soberly, according as God hath dealt to every man the measure of faith (Romans 12:3).

Father, I thank you that you have given to me the measure of faith I need to be exactly the kind of person you want me to be and to do all the things you want me to do. I praise you because we are all different and distinct individuals; yet you have given to each of us the same measure of faith as everyone else, so that I can take on the unique tasks that fit into your perfect plan for me. I thank you that you have given me just as much faith as anyone else in the world, because all your children are precious to you. I'm using and developing my measure of faith daily, right up to the hilt.

February 5

That the communication of thy faith may become effectual by the acknowledging of every good thing which is in you in Christ Jesus (Philemon 6).

My faith produces good fruit in me. Glory! It produces and promotes full recognition, appreciation, understanding, and precise knowledge of the fact that, when we identify ourselves with the ever-truthful God, who cannot deceive, our faith grows and multiplies and abounds. I praise you for a sound mind; for the salvation of my family; for health, wealth, and happiness; for joy, love, and peace; for prosperity and abundance. I praise you for every good thing. Glory!

February 6

I can do all things through Christ which strengtheneth me (Philippians 4:13).

Thank you for the faith to know that I am empowered through Jesus Christ to do *all things*. I thank you and praise you that I can handle any situation, because Jesus strengthens and equips me to succeed in even the most difficult situations and problems that come before me. Through Christ, every obstacle has become a stepping stone for me, every problem an opportunity. Through Christ, I have the will power to overcome any and all of my bad habits. I thank you because your Word doesn't say I can only do *some things* through Christ who strengthens me, but it says *I can do all things*. Hallelujah, that's power. I thank you that I can live in divine health. I thank you that I can live in prosperity. I thank you that I can live in total victory.

February 7

Now the just shall live by faith: but if any man draw back, my soul shall have no pleasure in him (Hebrews 10:38).

Glory to God, I'm living by faith. I praise you that your righteous servants shall live by the confident convictions we have regarding man's relationship to you and divine things. I thank you, Father, that we can believe in you, cleave to you, and trust in you. Because of this, we can rely wholly and continually on you through Jesus Christ. I bless you for the warning that, if we draw back, you will have no pleasure in us. Father, I'm living in faith, walking in faith, talking in faith, and running in faith, because I want to please you.

February 8

For by grace are ye saved through faith; and that not by yourselves: it is the gift of God (Ephesians 2:8).

I didn't have to save myself, hallelujah! I thank you, Father, that I didn't do a thing to deserve your unmerited favor, but because of your free grace I have been delivered from judgment and made a partaker of Christ's salvation. I thank you that it was a beautiful gift that you just gave to me, not something that I accomplished by my works or striving. Salvation is mine because you loved me so much that you sent your Son to save me from perishing in the darkness of sin and death. I thank you for that everlasting life I have in Christ. Because you have shown me the fullness of your love, *I love you, Father. I love your Son, Jesus Christ. I love the new life you have given me through your beloved Son.*

February 9

Giving thanks unto the Father, which hath made us meet to be partakers of the inheritance of the saints in light:

Who hath delivered us from the power of darkness, and hath translated us into the kingdom of his dear Son (Colossians 1:12, 13).

I will thank you and praise you forever, Father, because *I am delivered.* I've been taken out of the control and the dominion of darkness, changed so that I am qualified to share the inheritance of the saints, and translated into the kingdom of light. Glorious Father, how I praise you that, because of your loving-kindness and mercy, I have been made a partaker of the inheritance of all the saints. Glory, I've been delivered from bad habits, evil thoughts, and the very power of the devil. I want to say *thank you, thank you, thank you,* because you have reached inside me and turned me into a brand-new person. You have sent me straight into the Kingdom of your beloved Son, Jesus Christ!

February 10

Rejoice in the Lord always: and again I say, Rejoice (Philippians 4:4).

How can I thank you enough for all the wonderful reasons I have to rejoice in you, Father? I rejoice in your presence in my life. I rejoice in each new day you give me to live, to love, to enjoy, and to help others. I rejoice that I am your child and that you love me more than I love myself. I rejoice in your Word, in your power, in your glory. I rejoice in the blessings you shower upon me day after day—blessings of joy, of health, of prosperity, of family, and of friends. I rejoice in the work you give me to do and in the quiet times in my day when I come to you and worship you. I rejoice when I'm tired; I rejoice in you even when I am attacked by the devil. I delight in you even when my body is not up to par. I rejoice at night. I rejoice during the day. God, you are really fabulous.

February 11

Even the righteousness of God which is by faith of Jesus Christ unto all and upon all them that believe: for there is no difference (Romans 3:22).

Glory to God! I have the *righteousness of God* in me, because I have faith and personal trust in Jesus Christ. I praise you, Father, that your righteousness is available to everyone who believes in and confidently relies on Jesus, because that means I'm conformed to your Word and your promise. I'm rejoicing *right now* that I am marching in accordance with your plan. Thank you for filling me with your righteousness, because I'm using that loving righteousness with my family, my friends, and my colleagues. Father, I love your righteousness.

February 12

For I am persuaded, that neither death, nor life, nor angels, nor principalities, nor powers, nor things present, nor things to come, nor height, nor depth, nor any other creature, shall be able to separate us from the love of God, which is in Christ Jesus our Lord (Romans 8:38, 39).

Father, my faith is rising to new heights. I thank you that I am in your love and that nothing, *absolutely nothing, can ever separate me from your love.* I'm overwhelmed that your Word has made it so clear, so powerfully plain and positive, that I can never be moved from your love which is in Christ Jesus our Lord. Right this very second I rejoice that your power guarantees me your eternal love, no matter what the devil or any of his demons try to pull, no matter when or where. I'm living in your divine love, regardless of any and all circumstances.

February 13

I am crucified with Christ: nevertheless I live; yet not I, but Christ liveth in me: and the life which I now live in the flesh I live by the faith of the Son of God, who loved me, and gave himself for me (Galatians 2:20).

Glory to God. I'm dead and alive at the same time. Thank you, precious Father, that I'm living a life that is really Jesus Christ living in me. I praise you, Father, because my worldly ways and sins were crucified on the cross with Jesus, who loved me and gave himself for me. The old me is dead—doubts, thoughts, habits, hurts, and memories—and I'm a completely new person, top to bottom, inside and outside. The body life I live is now ruled by Jesus, and I live in this body of flesh and bone by my faith in him. Because of this, I'm a new person with nothing to hold me back. Father, I thank you that my new life glorifies you.

February 14

For God so loved the world, that he gave his only begotten Son, that whosoever believeth in him should not perish, but have everlasting life (John 3:16).

Father, this is the day the world says is the day for lovers, but I don't have to depend on just one day a year, because I'm living in your love every single day of the year. Thank you that your love encompasses the entire world and yet is personal just for me. I praise you because my Bible has my name in it and not just the words "the world." It actually has my name in it. Father, you said if I would simply believe in you, I would not perish, but have everlasting life. *I believe, I believe, I believe.* Thank you for the faith that lets me believe.

February 15

If any man speak, let him speak as the oracles of God; if any man minister, let him do it as of the ability which God giveth: that God in all things may be glorified through Jesus Christ, to whom be praise and dominion for ever and ever (I Peter 4:11).

Father, I bless you that as I speak, I speak as a prophet of God, because my mouth shall speak your words. I thank you that pleasant words are like a honeycomb, sweet to the soul and health to the bones. I praise you because I have a wholesome tongue, which is a tree of life; I bless you because my mouth is also as a well of life. I guard my tongue, so that I am not snared with the words of my mouth. My heart retains your words, and out of the abundance of my heart, filled with your words, shall I speak. Glory!

February 16

Casting all your care upon him; for he careth for you (I Peter 5:7).

Here are my cares, Father. This means *all* of my worries, anxieties, and concerns. I'm giving them all to you, once and for all. Your love overwhelms me. I praise and thank you for taking all my worries and cares away; because you love me so much, you don't want me to be burdened. My anxieties are *gone*. I bless you, because your Word works. Just as in the story of the prodigal son, you don't care what I've done or what I've been; you love me and care for me. Father, I'm so glad to be home at last with you. I rejoice because I'm your child, forgiven and restored by your mercy and loving-kindness to my inheritance in your kingdom. I praise you, Father, that my ways have been changed, because you care for me. Glory! I don't have any more worries.

February 17

A new heart also will I give you, and a new spirit will I put within you: and I will take away the stony heart out of your flesh, and I will give you an heart of flesh (Ezekiel 36:26).

Father, I'm so thankful that I have a new heart and a new spirit within me. Thank you, Father, that you've taken out my stony heart and replaced it with a heart filled to the brim with love. I love you. I love my friends. I love my family. I even love my enemies, because of what you have done for me. I never have to worry about running out of love, because you keep filling me up with more, more, more. I thank you, Father, that I can love you with all this new heart you've given me, and I thank you that with my new spirit I now live righteously.

February 18

Then spake Jesus again unto them saying, I am the light of the world: he that followeth me shall not walk in darkness, but shall have the light of life (John 8:12).

It's fun walking in the light, Father, because Jesus is the light of the world. Thank you, Father, for the light you gave me through your Son, Jesus, because by his wonderful, brilliant light I walked out of the gloom of darkness and left it behind forever. Now I can see the way, because the path of new life in Jesus shines with his wonderful light. I praise and glorify you, Father, for sending us the light of the world. Darkness holds no more fear for me, because it's gone from my life and I am walking and leaping and praising God in the light. I glory in the light of Jesus, and I follow where he leads me. In his light I am happy, I am healthy, I am prosperous. In his light I am fulfilled and victorious. His light *is* my life.

February 19

If any of you lack wisdom, let him ask of God, that giveth to all men liberally, and upbraideth not; and it shall be given him (James 1:5).

I praise you, Father, because I have wisdom. I have all the wisdom I need to prevail over any challenge, because your Word says if I don't have it, all I have to do is ask and it will be given to me by you, liberally and ungrudgingly. I thank you for giving me the kind of wisdom that triumphs over worldly knowledge every time, because worldly knowledge can't hold a candle to your wisdom. I thank you because you are a giving God, so I have all the wisdom I need to live and work and make decisions righteously and victoriously. I have wisdom in all my dealings, and I praise and thank you for it.

February 20

Let your conversation be without covetousness; and be content with such things as ye have: for he hath said, I will never leave thee, nor forsake thee. So that we may boldly say, The Lord is my helper, and I will not fear what man shall do unto me (Hebrews 13:5, 6).

I am gloriously satisfied, Father, in the overflowing abundance of divine blessings you have showered upon my life. I am content in your love. I praise you that there just isn't any room left in me for greed or envy of what my neighbors have, because your constant presence in my life is wealth far above the material things of this world. I'm not afraid of what anybody can do to me, because you've assured me that you are my Helper. Who could possibly prevail over my all-powerful God? Father, I don't have to rely on worldly security, because *you are everything I need.* I praise you because you never relax your hold on me. You never let me go. Hallelujah!

February 21

For verily I say unto you, That whosoever shall say unto this mountain, Be thou removed, and be thou cast into the sea; and shall not doubt it in his heart, but shall believe that those things which he saith shall come to pass; He shall have whatsoever he saith (Mark 11:23).

Father, I believe, I believe, I believe. Because I obey you, I believe from the bottom of my heart that your Word and your promises empower me to have anything I desire when I pray. What I say shall take place. Therefore, I say I have wisdom. I have health. I have happiness. I have prosperity. I have an abundance. I have joy. I have love. Father, I say to that mountain in my life, "Get lost and fall into the sea," because I believe your promise that I can have whatsoever I say. (Move your mountain right now.)

February 22

Therefore I say unto you, What things soever ye desire, when ye pray, believe that ye receive them, and ye shall have them (Mark 11:24).

Father, I believe *right now.* I've prayed, and the minute the words came out of my mouth, *I believed.* I thank you, Father, that you didn't tell me to wait until I built up enough faith to believe, but to believe the very instant I prayed, so that I could have the things that I desired. I praise you, *Father* that, because I take delight in you, you give me the desires of my heart, and that's why I know that I know that I *know* that you're going to fulfill the desires that you yourself have placed there. Glory, Father, thank you for the faith you've given to me.

February 23

If anyone is thirsty, let him come to me and drink. For the Scriptures declare that rivers of living water shall flow from the inmost being of anyone who believes in me (John 7:37, 38 LB).

Father, I'm thirsty, thirsty, thirsty. I'm drinking at your streams of living water deeper and deeper all the time. I bless you because that same river of living water that I'm drinking now blesses me and blesses everyone around me as it flows from my innermost being. Father, I praise you for giving to us a river of living water that never runs dry but keeps flowing and flowing. Thank you for that refilling station you've given me to use day and night. Thank you because it is open twenty-four hours a day. Father, I love you for that.

February 24

You can be very sure that the evil man will not go unpunished forever. And you can also be very sure that God will rescue the children of the godly (Proverbs 11:21 LB).

Father, how I praise you for such a promise. My faith is in you and not in what I see, because as I look at my children sometimes I feel like giving up. But you've promised that you will rescue my children, and how I love you for that. Thank you that my family is on your favored list, because you have promised that my household will be saved. I'm rejoicing in that. I thank you, Father, because *the wicked are overthrown, and are not; but the house of the righteous shall stand* (Proverbs 12:7). So my house is standing on the promises of your Word. I praise you that I am godly only because I have been born again of incorruptible seed. Hallelujah!

February 25

For this cause we also, since the day we heard it, do not cease to pray for you, and to desire that ye might be filled with the knowledge of his will in all wisdom and spiritual understanding: That ye might walk worthy of the Lord unto all pleasing, being fruitful in every good work, and increasing in the knowledge of God (Colossians 1:9, 10).

Father, I praise you that I am being filled with the knowledge of your will in all wisdom and spiritual understanding. I thank you that I am constantly learning your ways and purposes and that you are giving me discernment of spiritual things. I praise you that, because you have given me these blessings, I am walking worthy of you, Lord, being fruitful in every good work and steadily growing and increasing in my knowledge of you. I thank you that all my decisions are ordered by you. Glory!

February 26

And now I am coming to you. I have told them many things while I was with them so that they would be filled with my joy (John 17:13 LB).

Father, I bless you because I am filled with joy. The joy of the Lord is my strength, so I'm strong because my cup is filled to the top and overflowing with joy. I bless you because you have anointed me with the oil of gladness. I sing and shout with joy, because I have favor with God and man. Therefore, I'm always a winner. I bless you because my joy is contagious and flows over to reach others. Today I'm speaking love, joy, and peace to everyone I meet. Thank you for showing me the things that put joy in my heart. Glory, I'm bubbling, bubbling, bubbling over.

February 27

Being born again, not of corruptible seed, but of incorruptible, by the word of God, which liveth and abideth for ever (I Peter 1:23).

I'm born again of incorruptible seed. Father, I can't thank and praise you enough for lifting me out of the darkness and sin of the world, where mortal life leads only to death. By your Word I am made new, regenerated, reborn to eternal life in your Kingdom. I am in this world of corruption and decay, but I am not of it, because the perfect seed of your Word has made me into an entirely new person. Father, I praise you that your Word lives and abides forever. Because of this, I shall live forever, too. Glory!

February 28

The Spirit itself beareth witness with our spirit, that we are the children of God: and if children, then heirs; heirs of God, and joint-heirs with Christ (Romans 8:16, 17).

Father, how I thank you for letting me know in no uncertain terms that I can never be lost or alone, because the Holy Spirit says that I am your child. I know where I belong. Bless you, Father, that I am a joint-heir with Jesus, and you gave everything you had to him, so I share fully in the entire inheritance. Father, I'm so rich because of your promises. I praise you that, because I am a joint-heir with Jesus, I am your temple and your Spirit dwells in me. I thank you that I have power to overcome all obstacles in this world. You are my God, I am your child, and I claim your promise that all things in heaven and earth belong to me!

February 29

Therefore I say unto you, Take no thought for your life, what ye shall eat, or what ye shall drink; nor yet for your body, what ye shall put on. Is not the life more than meat, and the body than raiment? (Matthew 6:25).

Thank you, Father, for another beautiful month—a month when I had the opportunity to love you more than ever before; a month when I had the opportunity to study and grow in your Word. Father, your Word and your promises have become real in my life in ways that make me love you more and more. I thank you that your Word endures forever and that I have victory. I don't have to take thought for my life, because my life is in you, Father, and you supply *everything*. I thank you that the kingdom of God is not meat and drink, but righteousness and peace and joy in the Holy Ghost. I have health. I have prosperity. I have joy, I have peace. I have Jesus.

March

PROSPERITY

God spoke to me within seconds after I was saved. *He* spoke. I listened. I obeyed. It changed my life.

Did he tell me he loved me?

No! He had told me that before.

Did he tell me I was saved?

No!

Did he tell me my sins were forgiven?

No!

Did he tell me I was his child?

No!

He said very simply, "I want 20 percent of *everything* you've got." I don't believe I had ever given more than $5 in an offering in my entire life, and yet the very first thing God said to me after salvation was that he wanted my money.

I praise the Lord that I heard him and obeyed!

I never questioned the fact that it was God, and I never questioned whether or not I should be obedient. I just did it. I really thought he was charging me for my salvation (I didn't know my salvation was free), but I was so happy to be delivered from sin, I would have given him anything and everything I had.

Up until that time, money had been my god. Maybe that's why God spoke to me about the thing that needed to be changed the most.

I was completely ignorant of the Word of God. I didn't know that the Word says if you give, you are going to get it back. I didn't realize that there was a money-back guarantee in the Bible "signed" by God himself telling us what is going to happen when we learn to give to him.

I was ignorant of all these things because I had never read the Bible. That doesn't make any difference. God has to fulfill his Word—the good things and the bad—whether we know what it says or not. So God gave back to me, pressed down, shaken together, and running over (see Luke 6:38). I ended up with more than I started with, so I gave back to God, and he gave back to me.

Then I gave to him, and he gave to me, and I gave to him, and he gave to me again. I've been doing this for all the years I've been saved, and *I have never been able to outgive God.* I also know that I never will. And praise God, I have never had a need in my life since I learned to give to God.

God wants the same thing for you. He wants you to prosper and be in health. We live under the blessings of God and not under the curse. Confess and believe for prosperity this month.

March 1

Beloved, I wish above all things that thou mayest prosper and be in health, even as thy soul prospereth (III John 2).

My soul is prospering. Father, I rejoice that the wish you have for me, high above all others, is prosperity and health for both my body and my soul. Glory, how I thank you for being such a wonderful and loving Father, who takes care of me in such full and overflowing measure. Thank you for the secret of prosperity which lies in giving to you so that you can multiply it back to me. I'm not going to hold tight to what I have, Father, but instead I'm keeping my hands empty and open, so you can keep filling them up with more. And I'm placing the same trust in you for my health, Father, knowing how generously you provide. Thank you for the blessing of wonderful and divine health that I live in all this year. Your Word is my life, so my soul is prospering.

March 2

"Bring the whole tithe into the storehouse, that there may be food in my house. Test me in this," says the Lord Almighty, "and see if I will not throw open the floodgates of heaven and pour out so much blessing that you will not have room enough for it" (Malachi 3:10 NIV).

Here it is, Father, my whole tithe. I'm giving it to you. I praise you, Father, for being the best financial advisor I could possibly have. I'm giving generously into your storehouse, Almighty Father, because it pleases you to "throw open the floodgates of heaven" and let the blessings gush out in abundance upon us. I am made in your image, so I know you want me to be generous, even as you are generous in giving to me, until I have no room for more. I receive the gift of your blessed abundance with thanks and praise, and I'm giving to you, Father, fully trusting in your promise of return. I'm expanding my mind and my ability to receive your blessings to make more room for that flood that is pouring out of those flood-gates.

March 3

To the man who pleases him, God gives wisdom, knowledge and happiness, but to the sinner he gives the task of gathering and storing up wealth to hand it over to the one who pleases God (Ecclesiastes 2:26 NIV).

The sinner is my slave. Even if he owns a den of iniquity, he is working to gather and store up money to give to those who are in right standing with you, Father. Glory! I thank you that you have given me wisdom, knowledge, and happiness to know this. I rejoice because you teach us that covetousness and greed are meaningless. You take the wealth sinners have gained and give it to those who please you, for your way is righteousness. I receive that sinner's money right now. I'm blessed by your marvelous generosity, Father. Keep that sinner working, so I can have more to give to you.

March 4

Cast thy bread upon the waters: for thou shalt find it after many days (Ecclesiastes 11:1).

Heavenly Father, I love to cast my bread upon your waters and I praise you for the way you multiply it and send back many times over what I give. Thanks for showing me that the real secret of receiving is to give with a loving heart, because when I put my whole trust in you, everything always comes back magnified. Father, I thank you that I am able to give love, kindness, a helping hand, time, money, and gifts whenever you tell me to, because it's your good pleasure to replace all that I give from your own unlimited storehouse. I've cast my bread upon the water, Father, and I thank you for the cinnamon buns that are coming back. Thank you for the danish. Thank you for the doughnuts. Thank you that the whole bakery is coming back to me.

March 5

But seek ye first the kingdom of God, and his righteousness; and all these things shall be added unto you (Matthew 6:33).

All things? Father, I praise and thank you for the truth of the promises in your Word. You said *all things* shall be added to me, and I believe every word of it. I am craving and earnestly seeking everything in the Kingdom of God. You never fail me, for you have gathered me into your Kingdom and your righteousness. Here I am, jubilantly rejoicing because of it. You give me everything I need, not because of what I do or don't do, but because I'm a member of your very own family, loved and cared for from now through eternity. I hold out my hands to you, Father, and claim your promise that *all* things are added to me. I have love, joy, peace of mind, health, and prosperity. I have *all* things. Father, you're so good to me that I can't glorify you enough.

March 6

For the Lord God is a sun and shield: the Lord will give grace and glory: no good thing will he withhold from them that walk uprightly (Psalm 84:11).

I don't need sunglasses, Father, because you are my shield. I love you for promising that you will not withhold one single good thing from me. I rejoice to walk uprightly in your light, because in your light I can always know how to handle any situation. Your shield protects me from the devil's barbs, his lies, his deceits, and I rejoice that he runs at breakneck speed away from your light. Protected by your shield, illumined by your light, my life is blessed by an abundance of your gifts, for you are a God of grace and glory. I glorify your name, Father, because you supply all my needs and more. Thank you for the heavenly bliss and favor you generously bestow on me. I confidently commit all I am and all I have to you.

March 7

Give, and it shall be given unto you; good measure, pressed down, and shaken together, and running over, shall men give into your bosom. For with the same measure that ye mete withal it shall be measured to you again (Luke 6:38).

Father, how I bless you for your money-back guarantee that says when I give to you, it shall be given back to me. When I give love, you give me an exceeding abundance of love. When I give time, you return that time to me over and over again. When I give money, you give it back to me in full and in overflowing and plenteous amounts. I praise you that you use what I give as a measuring spoon to dish out what you give to me, so I don't ever need to be limited by anything except what I am willing to give. Father, I'm giving you my all—everything I am and all I own—and I thank you that I am walking in a superabundant supply.

March 8

But remember this—if you give little, you will get little. A farmer who plants just a few seeds will get only a small crop, but if he plants much, he will reap much (II Corinthians 9:6 LB).

How I praise you, Father, for the wonderful harvest you are bringing forth in my garden. Thank you for teaching me how to be a successful farmer. Thank you for teaching me to sow generously and joyfully in great abundance, so you can bless it and return it to me multiplied beyond my wildest dreams. Thank you for the harvest you have prepared for me. Thank you for teaching me not to be stingy in any area of my life, whether it's in love, health, joy, or finances. I plant in faith, generously—and you open the floodgates of heaven to pour blessings on me. I thank and praise you, Father, for the exploding abundance of all things you bring about from the seeds of my giving.

March 9

Do not gather and heap up and store for yourselves treasures on earth, where moth and rust and worm consume and destroy, and where thieves break through and steal; But gather and heap up and store for yourselves treasures in heaven, where neither moth nor rust nor worm consume and destroy, and where thieves do not break through and steal; For where your treasure is, there will your heart be also (Matthew 6:19-21 Amp.).

No thanks, I don't need any mothballs today. I'm not storing my treasures up here on the earth, but I'm storing them up in heaven with you, Father, where I don't have to worry about moths and rust or even thieves who break through and steal. Father, I'm banking my treasure with you, because you are the most reliable trust company in the entire world. You are a living river of blessings, and I praise you for taking care of your children with loving interest. My treasure is in heaven with you, and my heart is right up there too.

March 10

But my God shall supply all your need according to his riches in glory by Christ Jesus (Philippians 4:19).

My needs are gloriously and liberally supplied. Thank you, Father, for sending Jesus to die on the cross as a ransom for my sins, because through him I have abundant new life. I praise you not only for paying all my bills, but also for taking care of me in countless invisible ways—providing love when I need it, lifting my spirits, sending a friend when I need a helping hand, directing your angels to guard my family. Over and over again, you surprise me with your miraculous timing in providing answers to even unspoken prayers of mine. Father, I rejoice that my needs are faithfully and constantly fulfilled from your wonderful and inexhaustible riches in glory by Christ Jesus.

March 11

And the barrel of meal wasted not, neither did the cruse of oil fail, according to the word of the Lord, which he spake by Elijah (I Kings 17:16).

My cruse of oil shall never fail, because I shall never eat my seed. I praise you, Father, that when the widow was willing to listen to your prophet and share what she had instead of eating it all herself, you kept filling the barrel of meal and pouring oil into the cruse. Father, how we bless you for giving us instructions on how to save sufficient at all times. I praise you that, even though the supply looks low at times, I can rest assured that you're always there to put in what I need.

March 12

I love them that love me; and those that seek me early shall find me. Riches and honour are with me; yea, dura-

ble riches and righteousness. My fruit is better than gold, yea, than fine gold; and my revenue than choice silver. I lead in the way of righteousness, in the midst of the paths of judgment: That I may cause those that love me to inherit substance; and I will fill their treasures (Proverbs 8:17-21).

Father, how I love your Word and all the promises you have for me. I thank you that enduring wealth and uprightness in every area and relationship as well as right standing with you are mine. I thank you that you even allow me to inherit substance, often from sources I never knew about, and that you fill my treasures, so that I am indeed wealthy, because my riches are heavenly and divine. Thank you that you have taken charge of my earthly bank account and filled it with divine deposits. Glory!

March 13

The curse of the Lord is in the house of the wicked; but he blesseth the habitation of the just (Proverbs 3:33).

Father, my house is blessed. I rejoice that you are a God of justice, that no thought or act escapes your notice, that you know which are the houses of the wicked and which are the houses of the righteous. You see through all the deceptions of the wicked; there is no way they can hide from your curse. But I praise you that you also see directly into the hearts and minds of the righteous and that you never forget to bless and reward your children who serve you faithfully. Look into my heart and my mind, dear Father, because I rejoice in praising you. I glory in your wonderful blessings.

March 14

The blessing of the Lord, it maketh rich, and he addeth no sorrow with it (Proverbs 10:22).

I praise you, Father, for filling my life with the treasure of your blessing, which makes me rejoice day after day. I am rich in you. I am rich in your endless love, which feeds me like manna from heaven. You put the food on my table, the clothes on my back, the smiles on my children's faces. Glory, Father, how can I thank you enough? You give me health, happiness, and prosperity. You guard me from temptation and teach me with the wisdom of your Word. You renew and refresh my spirit, so I can face each day with joy. Father, I praise you for not adding sorrow to my life, because with all your blessings, there just isn't room for it.

March 15

And I say unto you, Ask and it shall be given you; seek, and ye shall find; knock and it shall be opened unto you. For every one that asketh receiveth; and he that seeketh findeth; and to him that knocketh it shall be opened (Luke 11:9, 10).

Glory hallelujah, Father, I'm an asker, a seeker, and a knocker, and because of this, I'm a receiver. Thank you that your Word says if I ask it shall be given to me. Thank you that you didn't say *some* will receive, but you said *every one*, and that includes me. Father, I praise you because when I ask, *you* give to me; when I knock, *you* open the door; when I seek, *you* guide me safely to my destination. I'm asking, Father, and therefore I have what I ask for. I have love. I have joy. I have health. I have prosperity. Thank you for being such a loving and generous Father to me.

March 16

He hath given meat unto them that fear him: he will ever be mindful of his covenant (Psalm 111:5).

O glorious Father, you are the river of life, the Provider of all my well-being. I rejoice every day, because you remember me without fail. You not only put the meat on my table, but you nourish my soul and protect me from all physical harm, because I am your child and you love me. I eat the meat you give me with a hearty appetite, delighting in each bite, because I know who has provided it and who will always provide it. Father, I am thankful for everything you give me, for it all belongs to you, and I am blessed by your caring, sharing, loving, wonderful faithfulness to me. Hallelujah! I praise you that your covenant is forever imprinted on your mind, so that you will remember it throughout all eternity.

March 17

The Lord is my shepherd; I shall not want (Psalm 23:1).

I shall not want for health. I shall not want for finances. Father, do you know what gets me so excited about your promises? They are magnificent, *big* promises. You just don't give out small, stingy promises to your children, because your *love for us is so great that you want us to have the whole works.* I thank you and praise you, heavenly Father, because you say plainly and clearly that I *shall not* want. You are my God, and I am your child. You are my Shepherd, and I follow where you lead. I rejoice because you are the kind of Father who wants me to prosper in this life and to share your eternal glory in the next. Father, I'm blessed beyond words. I shall not want for joy. I shall not want for happiness. Glory!

March 18

Blessed be the Lord, who daily loadeth us with benefits, even the God of our salvation. Selah (Psalm 68:19).

I'm loaded, but not with problems, Father. I thank you for loading me with the good things of life every day. I don't have to live on yesterday's blessings or wait for tomorrow's blessings, because you send fresh new blessings each day. I'm singing and shouting my praises up to you, because you give me a taste of heaven right on this earth. You are the God of my salvation, and all glory belongs to you. Every moment of this day is special to me, because you are always right here with me, and you know what benefits I need much better than I do. I love you, praise you, and bless your name, Father, for all I'm receiving today. It's all so good, you can just keep loading me down. Thank you that I don't have to have monthly or weekly blessings, but that you supply them on a daily basis. Hallelujah!

March 19

Yea, the Lord shall give that which is good; and our land shall yield her increase (Psalm 85:12).

I can't help praising you, Father, because you know how to give good gifts. You have given me life, and you have removed the curse of sin from my life through the sacrifice of your only begotten Son on the cross. I thank you for my new life and my salvation. I thank you for Jesus Christ. I thank you for the Holy Spirit. Yes, Father, you give what is good, and my heart rejoices. My arms open wide to receive your gifts. I love you with all my heart, all my soul, all my mind, and all my strength. Because of your goodness, Father, our land is blessed with a rich harvest, and I am prospered.

March 20

And all these blessings shall come upon you and overtake you, if you heed the voice of the Lord your God (Deuteronomy 28:2 Amp.).

I'm ready, Father, to be overcome and overtaken with blessings. I've listened to the devil too long, but from now on I'm listening to your voice only. I've cleaned out my ears, and I'm hearing even the tiniest little word you say to me. I'm singing your praises and rejoicing because you've promised that your blessings will catch up with me and simply overwhelm me. I can hardly wait. I want to peek over my shoulder and watch them arrive, Father, because, since Jesus took my sins away so that I might be restored to your favor, I've inherited even the blessings you gave to Abraham. I praise you for the abiding love you have for your people, which has flowed down through the centuries to reach me. I bless you because I live under your blessings. I heard the condition to your blessings, too, Father, so I'm doing my part and following your instructions completely.

March 21

Blessed shall you be in the city, and blessed shall you be in the field (Deuteronomy 28:3 Amp.).

Heavenly Father, you know what our cities are like, and you know what it's like to be a farmer these days, so I rejoice that your blessing follows me wherever I go. I thank you that you are my shield and protection from evil in the city. I thank you that you are my strength and my rest in the field. You are with me wherever I go, so that my way is blessed and prosperous, my work goes well, and my life bears fruit that pleases you. Because you love and bless me, I am not swallowed up in the confusion and darkness of the world. I rejoice, Father, because you are with me.

March 22

Blessed shall be your basket and your kneading trough (Deuteronomy 28:5 Amp.).

How I rejoice, Father, that I don't have to worry about inflation, the price of food and shopping. I praise you that complex economic policies, the rise and fall of the stock market, and business red tape don't have any effect on your blessings. Heavenly Father, when you say my basket is blessed, *it is blessed.* When you say my store is blessed, *it is blessed.* My kneading trough, or my bread, is blessed because I'm feasting on Jesus, the Bread of life. Your blessings come as promises, *in power and in truth.* You are my God, and nations rise and decay under your hand, but your blessings remain with me through thick and thin. Father, I've forgotten how to worry, because I'm too busy praising and thanking you to have time for it.

March 23

Blessed shall you be when you come in, and blessed shall you be when you go out (Deuteronomy 28:6 Amp.).

I'm blessed coming in, and I'm blessed going out. Glory, Father, when I knock on the door, you open it so I can come in—and I am blessed. When I go out to seek, you help me to find what I'm seeking, and again I'm blessed. Father, only through you am I assured of getting blessed whether I'm coming or going. I praise you, heavenly Father, *for directing my way,* because in your glorious wisdom I am guided to the door of opportunities that bless me, and I am guided out the door to better opportunities that bless me again. I rejoice and thank you, Father, that you care for me enough to always bless my coming in and going out.

March 24

The Lord shall cause your enemies who rise up against you to be defeated before your face; they shall come out against you one way, and flee before you seven ways (Deuteronomy 28:7 Amp.).

Enemies, get ready to go. I thank you, Father, that those who come against me with evil in their hearts will never find me alone, but always with you. I praise you because in your righteousness and power, you defeat my enemies and strike confusion into their ranks, so that they run before me seven different ways. Father, even when I am under attack, I'm still blessed, because I stand firm and glorify you before the world for causing the defeat of unrighteousness. Thank you, heavenly Father, for blessing me under all conditions. I can't lose with you, Father, because I'm blessed when they attack me, or when they leave me alone.

March 25

The Lord shall command the blessing upon you in your storehouse, and in all that you undertake; and He will bless you in the land which the Lord your God gives you (Deuteronomy 28:8 Amp.).

Everything I undertake is blessed—what a promise. Father, I praise you because when you command something to be done, *it is done.* Thank you for commanding a blessing upon me for the projects I've already started and those I'm going to do in the future. Father, I work with your praises upon my lips, because you bless and reward those who are faithful to you. I don't worry about my savings, because your blessing protects what is mine better than any bank vault. I'm not anxious about the success of anything I tackle, because under your blessing my work prospers. Father, you have blessed me in everything you have given me, and I am grateful to you. Hallelujah!

March 26

And the Lord shall make you have a surplus of prosperity, through the fruit of your body, of your livestock, and of your ground, in the land which the Lord swore to your fathers to give you (Deuteronomy 28:11 Amp.).

Thank you, Father, that your Word promises more than bare sufficiency; your Word promises *plenteous goods*. I rejoice and praise you because your plan for me is a life of abundance, not just scraping by day to day. I thank you because everything I do multiplies and bears fruit in the power of your generous and loving blessing upon me and upon my land. Father, you are a fountain of blessings to me, and I glorify your name. I have more than enough, and I will always have an excess, an oversupply, and a balance left over to give to others in need. Hallelujah!

March 27

The Lord shall open to you His good treasury . . . (Deuteronomy 28:12 Amp.).

Father, when I think that you open to me your good treasury, that means everything you've got is open and available to me. I feel like a child, full of excitement, sticking my hand in a grab bag of goodies. Some things in a grab bag are disappointing, but, Father, *all* the things in your treasury are good. I rejoice because it is truly your pleasure to give me the Kingdom. I bless you, Father, because when you open something up, you don't open it just a little crack or a little chink, but you open up the whole thing. I thank you and rejoice that you are the one who's doing it, Father, and that you don't make me try to chisel my way inside of something difficult to get into. You just open it up to me, free of charge. How I love you for your generosity.

March 28

A good man leaves an inheritance (of moral stability and goodness) to his children's children, and the wealth of the sinner (finds its way eventually) into the hands of the righteous, for whom it was laid up (Proverbs 13:22 Amp.).

Heavenly Father, I thank you that I am leaving an inheritance of moral values and good behavior to my children and my children's children, both through the example I set for them and through teaching them your Word. I glorify you, Father, because you don't allow the sinner's ways to go unpunished, for you take the sinner's money and pass it into the hands of those who love you. You are a God of justice and righteousness, because your Word says, *the wages of sin is death,* and you bring the sinner's inheritance to nothing. Father, I lift my hands up right now to be a funnel for you to pour the sinner's wealth into me, and I receive your prosperity.

March 29

Roll your works upon the Lord—commit and trust them wholly to Him; (He will cause your thoughts to become agreeable to His will, and) so shall your plans be established and succeed (Proverbs 16:3 Amp.).

My plans are established and succeeding. What a promise. I praise you, Father, because when I bring my intentions and plans and ideas to you before I start on any project, you conform my thoughts to your will, so that everything I do succeeds wonderfully. I thank you because even if I come to you with wrong ideas and roll them all upon you, trusting and committing them to your precious care, you just turn my thoughts around, so that I think in the right direction. I'm letting all my thoughts go right straight to you, because without you my thoughts could go off on all kinds of tangents and get me into trouble, but with you my plans are established and succeeding. Hallelujah!

March 30

No weapon that is formed against thee shall prosper; and every tongue that shall rise against thee in judgment thou shalt condemn. This is the heritage of the servants of the Lord, and their righteousness is of me, saith the Lord (Isaiah 54:17).

Father, I rejoice that my heritage in you protects me from the weapons of enemies and the tongues of the wicked or mistaken people who speak against me. My righteousness is in you, so I have nothing to fear. The devil and his deceptions are turned away from me and are brought to nothing by your power, because my faith is in you. You are my shield and my buckler. Thank you for wrapping your shield of faith around me, so that I can confidently face the world and know that no weapon of any kind that is formed against me can prosper in any way because of your Word and your Spirit. Glory!

March 31

So shall my word be that goeth forth out of my mouth: it shall not return unto me void, but it shall accomplish that which I please, and it shall prosper in the thing whereto I sent it (Isaiah 55:11).

Glory, Father, that your Word goes forth with *power, and does what you intend it to do.* I thank you because your promises and your blessings prosper me and my works, exactly as you want them to. I thank you for your loving-kindness, for the many blessings you have poured out upon me this month, and for your constant presence in my life. I praise you because you are a God of power and glory and righteousness, and because the Word that goes forth from your mouth with such wonderful authority brings me joy, peace, love, happiness, friendship, health, and prosperity as I let those same words flow through my mouth.

April

THE NAME OF JESUS

Confess this every day this month, along with the one for each particular day, to firmly establish in your mind that *he is risen!*

> Thank you, Father, that we can say *he is risen* because when they went to the tomb, he was not there. It was *empty.* Thank you that in spite of the fact that he died on the cross and took *all* the sins and filth of mankind upon himself, he established forever that the *name of Jesus* was above all other names when he arose victoriously out of the bonds of hell and over the power of Satan. Thank you, Father, for the resurrection power that made salvation possible.

Each day as you say your devotion, whether you are alone or with someone, say it out loud, and say it with authority, until the devotion that is written becomes *your* devotion.

April 1

Wherefore God also hath highly exalted him, and given him a name which is above every name: That at the name of Jesus every knee should bow, of things in heaven, and things in earth, and things under the earth; And that every tongue should confess that Jesus Christ is Lord, to the glory of God the Father (Philippians 2:9-11).

Jesus, Jesus, Jesus. How I love that name. I bless you, Father, for giving your Son such a beautiful name. Thank you for the power in that name. I praise you that the name of Jesus is over and above sickness, disease, poverty, demons, and everything else the devil tries to give me. I take the name of Jesus over any plague that tries to come near my dwelling, because that name is above all things inside and outside. My tongue confesses daily that Jesus Christ is Lord. Jesus is Lord. *Jesus is Lord.*

April 2

And he arose, and rebuked the wind, and said unto the sea, Peace, be still. And the wind ceased, and there was a great calm (Mark 4:39).

Father, how we bless you that, at the name of Jesus, the wildest storm that may be blowing around us has to be still and quiet. I praise you that when that old enemy comes in, like a flood, the name of Jesus muzzles whatever the devil is trying to do. My heart shall have peace all day today, because whenever the wind starts to blow again, I shall take the name of Jesus on my lips. Thank you for the peace that passes all understanding that rests in my heart because of what you've given to us in the name of Jesus.

April 3

That the name of our Lord Jesus Christ may be glorified in you, and ye in him, according to the grace of our God and the Lord Jesus Christ (II Thessalonians 1:12).

Father, it has been nearly 2,000 years since you sent your Son to walk on this earth. I'm bubbling over and still can't stop talking about this wonderful, miraculous life, and I still can't thank you and praise you enough for sending him. I thank and praise you for giving me the opportunity to have Jesus glorified in me by the way I live my life before all the world, and to be glorified even myself, because I live in him. Thank you, Father, because this can only happen by your grace and that of our Lord Jesus Christ. Thank you for that beautiful name above all names—the name of Jesus. I take it upon my lips daily in thanksgiving for what you have done for me.

April 4

And the whole multitude sought to touch him: for there went virtue out of him, and he healed them all (Luke 6:19).

He healed them all. What a statement, and what a truth! I praise you and exalt the name of Jesus, because Jesus and his name are one, Father. There was so much power in his very being, his presence, that the ever-present virtue flowed out of him, healing every person. I bless you because you have given me the same power and authority to use the name of Jesus so that healing virtue can flow out of me. I praise you that Jesus was victorious in all circumstances and at all times; therefore, because I am a joint heir with him, I am victorious and triumphant at all times because of that name. *Jesus.* Name above all names. I say it out loud.

April 5

And in that day ye shall ask me nothing. Verily, verily, I say unto you, Whatsoever ye shall ask the Father in my name, he will give it you. Hitherto have ye asked nothing in my name: ask, and ye shall receive, that your joy may be full (John 16:23, 24).

Your goodness is almost impossible to believe. My joy is full and running all over the place. I thank you, Father, that Jesus said *whatever* I ask in his *name*, you will give to me. I rejoice and give thanks that the name of Jesus has so much power and authority. I'm blessed to ask in the name of Jesus because of the love that fills my heart when his name is on my lips and because of the sweet expectation of receiving what I ask from you, Father. Thank you for giving so bountifully in my life that my joy is running over.

April 6

Ye have not chosen me, but I have chosen you, and ordained you, that ye should go and bring forth fruit, and that your fruit should remain: that whatsoever ye shall ask of the Father in my name, he may give it you (John 15:16).

You chose me. You ordained me. You picked me out, because you wanted to. I thank you, Father, that I am chosen and ordained through Jesus Christ to bear fruit in my life from the love and truth he expresses in me. Thank you that I live so that people can see the love of Jesus in me and that I can reach out to tell the Good News to others. Thank you that I am appointed to bring forth fruit and that my fruit will remain as your Word says. Thank you that I can ask for anything in Jesus' name, and you will give it to me.

April 7

Verily, verily, I say unto you, He that believeth on me, the works that I do shall he do also; and greater works than these shall he do; because I go unto my Father. And whatsoever ye shall ask in my name, that will I do, that the Father may be glorified in the Son. If ye shall ask anything in my name, I will do it (John 14:12-14).

I believe on you; I do believe on you. And I get so excited when I read that I can do even greater things than Jesus did. My mind can't comprehend all the things you've promised; but, Father, I believe them, because you have said so in your Word. I bless you that your Word makes such a complete and total statement in using the word *whatsoever. Whatsoever* I ask in the name of Jesus will be done. I want to glorify your Son Jesus in all that I do. I'm walking in power because you said so.

April 8

Then Peter said unto them, Repent, and be baptized every one of you in the name of Jesus Christ for the remission of sins, and ye shall receive the gift of the Holy Ghost (Acts 2:38).

Father, I rejoice and thank you for the power that's in the name of Jesus. I thank you that at that name the lame shall walk, the blind shall see, and healings shall take place today just as they did in the days when the disciples walked on this earth. I thank you for the blessings that the name of Jesus brings. Thank you for the gift of the Holy Spirit, for the power that comes with the Holy Spirit, for the joy that comes with the Holy Spirit. I praise you, Father, that you give *all* your blessings to *all* your children. I'm not going to miss a single one.

April 9

And these signs shall follow them that believe; In my name shall they cast out devils; they shall speak with new tongues (Mark 16:17).

Glorious Father, how I praise and thank you that in the *name* of Jesus I have power over devils. They all know who he is, and I don't have to fear them one bit, because the devil himself trembles at the very name of Jesus. Thank you, Father, that all the powers of darkness are afraid and run away at the mention of Jesus, because through him they and their deceptions and sneaky, evil plans are defeated. What a blessing you give to us, Jesus, when we speak with new tongues. Thank you, Father, for the language of love you give us with which to praise you and love you. Thank you that this is for all believers, and that includes *me*. Thank you for these two signs.

April 10

They shall lay hands on the sick, and they shall recover (Mark 16:18).

Thank you, Father, that as I look at my hands I don't see anything powerful, I don't see anything unusual, I don't see much of anything except fingers on each hand. But your Word says that in the *name of Jesus*, these ordinary hands can be laid on sick people, and *the sick shall recover.* I praise you for not saying *may* be used or that only some hands would be used, but you simply said that the hands of believers *would* be used. I'm a believer, Father, and, even though I might not be able to feel power flowing through my hands at all times, by faith in your Word, I know it's there, and I know that the sick *shall* recover when my hands are laid upon them. Thank you that my family is made whole by the use of my hands.

April 11

And they called them, and commanded them not to speak at all nor teach in the name of Jesus. . . . Saying, Did not we straitly command you that ye should not teach in this name? and, behold, ye have filled Jerusalem with your doctrine, and intend to bring this man's blood upon us. Then Peter and the other apostles answered and said, We ought to obey God rather than men (Acts 4:18; 5:28, 29).

Thank you, Father, that the *name* of Jesus has so much power that the devil and his cohorts flee at its very mention. I thank you that the Sadducees were so afraid of the power at the mention of the name of Jesus that they forbade Peter and John to ever speak of his name. Thank you for their boldness in saying "We ought to obey God rather than men." I praise you that I can use that same boldness today and say the exact same words and that I'm a God-pleaser and not a people-pleaser. Bless you for the power in that name.

April 12

And they that went before, and they that followed, cried, saying, Hosanna; Blessed is he that cometh in the name of the Lord (Mark 11:9).

Father, I thank you that I come in the name of the Lord, because I am a child of God, redeemed by the blood of the Lamb, the sacrifice of Jesus Christ on the cross, and because of the word of my testimony. I rejoice and praise you, Father, that because I come in his name, I am blessed. Thank you for sending your Son, Jesus, to prepare the way for us to follow him. Hosanna, I'm singing and shouting his praises, because I come in his name.

April 13

Heaven and earth shall pass away, but my words shall not pass away (Matthew 24:35).

Father, it is beyond my comprehension that this earth will someday pass away, and that the sun, moon, and stars that I've seen and been used to all my life, will pass away. But I believe it because your Word says so. I rejoice that the things of your eternal Kingdom shall not pass away, and that you have chosen me to spend eternity in your glorious Kingdom because of my salvation in Jesus Christ. How I thank you for sending your Son to us, and how I praise you for giving me your Word to stand on all the days of my life. My spirit is lifted up to heavenly places when I think of these wonderful promises.

April 14

Behold, I give unto you power to tread on serpents and scorpions, and over all the power of the enemy: and nothing shall by any means hurt you (Luke 10:19).

That is real power, Father. I thank you because Jesus unreservedly gave us the power to walk over snakes and scorpions without harm. I thank you that this power was magnified to give us power over the enemy, without possibility of retaliation upon us, because Jesus guaranteed that nothing would be able to hurt us. I praise you, Father, because Jesus didn't limit our power to particular conditions, and he didn't say we only had power over part of the enemy but over *all* the enemy's power. Thank you, Father, that nothing is going to hurt us, because Jesus gave us that power in his name.

April 15

Verily I say unto you, Whosoever shall not receive the kingdom of God as a little child shall in no wise enter therein (Luke 18:17).

Glory, Father, I'm so thankful because getting into your Kingdom is so simple that I'm going to shout out your praises. What a blessing that I am not required to have a college degree. I don't even have to speak Greek or Hebrew, and I don't have to belong to a certain club or be an expert in anything. I'm so glad that you let me join your special club just by simple faith in the blood of Jesus. I didn't come in by intellect or meditation or muscles. There wasn't anything to figure out; I didn't have to buy a ticket; there was no red tape. How I praise you, Father, that you sent Jesus to show me the way.

April 16

And he said, The things which are impossible with men are possible with God (Luke 18:27).

That's the epitome of an impossible statement, Father, because many times we're limited by what science says. We've been taught that if science can't solve a problem or heal a disease, it can't be done. I praise you, Father, because there is an infinitely greater hope, an infinitely greater power, than science. Jesus said it; I believe it; and it's so. The very things that are impossible with men are possible with you. Thank you, Father, that through you I can expect the impossible and the miraculous to happen. You are the changeless God. You are the same God of miracles today as you were 2,000 years ago, or in Moses' time, or at the creation. Bless you that you are *my* Father!

April 17

For the Son of man is come to seek and to save that which was lost (Luke 19:10).

He searched for me; he hunted me; he pursued me; he sought me. Thank you, Father, for sending your very own Son, Jesus, to rescue me when I was lost in the darkness of sin. I thank you that you loved me so much, you let your own Son bear my sins upon the cross, so that I might be cleansed and saved from eternal damnation. I was lost, but he found me and saved me, so I could become part of your Kingdom. I rejoice that Jesus shined his light on the path that led me right to your gate. Father, I will praise you and glorify your name forever, because your Son was sacrificed so I could have eternal life. Thank you, Father!

April 18

For the joy of the Lord is your strength (Nehemiah 8:10).

Jesus gives joy! Glory to God, how I sing hosanna to the Highest because of the joy that overflows in my heart. I praise you that the redeemed of the Lord shall return and come with singing unto Zion, and everlasting joy shall be upon their heads. How I praise you that they shall obtain gladness and joy, and sorrow and sighing shall flee away. I can rejoice because my name is written in heaven. Father, I thank you for the beautiful words of the angel when he said, *Behold, I bring you good tidings of great joy!* Thank you that the Good News was Jesus and the good tidings still bring joy today. Father, I'm walking and leaping and praising you because of the overabundance of joy in my heart.

April 19

If the Son therefore shall make you free, ye shall be free indeed. . . . Verily, verily, I say unto you, if a man keep my saying, he shall never see death (John 8:36; 51).

I'm free, I'm free, I'm free, for whoever the Son sets free is *free indeed!* I am liberated; I am unconditionally set free! I am unquestionably set free! Glory, Father, I thank you for the freedom I have in this beautiful country of ours, but I thank you much more for the freedom Jesus came to bring me. Thank you that you sent Jesus to free me from bondage to sin and to free me from death, which your Word says is the wages of sin. I rejoice and praise your name, Father, because now I shall never see spiritual death. I have a glorious eternal life ahead of me, and I'm enjoying it right this very minute. Thank you, Father. Hallelujah!

April 20

The thief cometh not, but for to steal, and to kill, and to destroy: I am come that they might have life, and that they might have it more abundantly (John 10:10).

I hate the devil. He's a robber, a crook, a pirate, a burglar, and a good-for-nothing. He steals, he robs, he plunders, he hijacks, he swindles, he blackmails, he cheats, and he tries to destroy everything that comes his way. Father, how I love you that Jesus came to give me the abundant life by restoring me to your love, the source of all abundance. I thank you that the devil, who comes as a thief, is powerless to steal the new life I have in you, because he has to run from the very name of Jesus. Thank you, Father, for my new life of abundance—love, peace, joy, health, prosperity, and *eternal life in your Kingdom*. Hallelujah!

April 21

Verily, verily, I say unto you, Except a corn of wheat fall into the ground and die, it abideth alone; but if it die, it bringeth forth much fruit (John 12:24).

I see a whole wheat field, Father, swaying in the breeze of the Holy Spirit. How I thank you that Jesus died on the cross and rose again the third day, to bring forth the fruit of salvation in us so we might have eternal life in your kingdom. I thank you that I'm part of that fruit crop. If that one kernel had not died, Father, there would have never been a way for me to have eternal life. My sins were washed away in the blood of the Lamb you sent as a living sacrifice for me. I rejoice because I'm a *new person* living a *new life* in your love, and all this was made possible through one precious kernel—your lovely Son, Jesus.

April 22

And such were some of you: but ye are washed, but ye are sanctified, but ye are justified in the name of the Lord Jesus, and by the Spirit of our God (I Corinthians 6:11).

Father, how I praise you that I have been washed absolutely clean and spotless by Jesus' complete atonement for sin and made pure and free from the guilt of sin. Thank you that I am set apart, consecrated, purified, sanctioned, and authorized in that name that is above all names. I praise you that I have been pronounced righteous, and that all the things you held against me before I was saved are now just as if they had never happened. I take that wonderful name upon my lips at all times and tell the world about the wonderful things that happen in that name!

April 23

Peace I leave with you, my peace I give unto you: not as the world giveth, give I unto you. Let not your heart be troubled, neither let it be afraid (John 14:27).

Your peace is certainly different from the world's, Father. I rejoice and thank you for that very special kind of peace that Jesus gave me. I praise you that I don't have to be agitated and disturbed by happenings in the world, because that's not the kind of peace you give. That special peace is a divine peace. It calms my heart and mind in exactly the same manner as when Jesus calmed a storm for his fearful disciples in a boat. I praise you, Father, that nothing and no one can ever trouble my heart or take away the peace that Jesus gave me, because it's divine and it's mine.

April 24

If ye abide in me, and my words abide in you, ye shall ask what ye will, and it shall be done unto you (John 15:7).

Jesus, I'm abiding in you. I'm vitally united to you through your Word, and I'm letting your Word settle down deep inside me, into all the dark corners of my life, so that they will permanently dwell, reside, live, and stay within me at all times. I'm speaking your Word; I'm saying your Word; I'm living your Word; I'm loving your Word. I'm blessed and thankful to be always with you and your abiding love, to be able to ask *anything* of you and know that it will be done. Father, I praise you and bless you, because you are always there to provide answers to my problems, to love me, nourish me, and lift me up. I'm soaring higher and higher all the time, because I'm abiding in you and you're abiding in me.

April 25

To whom God would make known what is the riches of the glory of this mystery among the Gentiles; which is Christ in you, the hope of glory (Colossians 1:27).

Thank you, Father, that you have made known to me what once was a mystery to the Gentiles, because the mystery is simply that Jesus Christ lives right inside me. I praise you because, with Jesus inside me, I have the riches of glory, the power to live righteously in this world, and the hope of eternal life in your Kingdom. Thank you, Father, that it pleases you to make this mystery known to me, so I can live by faith in your grace through Jesus Christ and let my light shine before mankind. I don't know how Jesus can live in me, Father, and that's not important! The important thing is that he does!

April 26

And have put on the new man, which is renewed in knowledge after the image of him that created him . . . Put on therefore, as the elect of God, holy and beloved, bowels of mercies, kindness, humbleness of mind, meekness, longsuffering (Colossians 3:10, 12).

I'm sparkling, I'm clean, I'm shiny, and I'm new. Father, thank you that I am a new person in Christ, with a new spiritual self that is continually being renewed and perfected in knowledge, after the image of my Creator. Thank you that I'm being sanctified and made holy as one of your elect, because to do your works I've been given your characteristics—mercy, kindness, humility, meekness, patience, and willingness to endure whatever comes before me. Thank you, Father, for your love, because these things would never be mine in the flesh, but they are mine because of you.

April 27

For God hath not called us into uncleanness, but unto holiness (I Thessalonians 4:7).

I praise you, Father, for your Word which says loud and clear that my calling is not just a part-time job, where I can do your holy work part of the time and fool around with sin at other times. Thank you that you want *all* of me *all* the time. I praise you that I don't have unclean desires and thoughts, because you protect and shield me from the filth that the devil throws at me. Thank you, Father, that, as I follow Jesus Christ and abide in him, the power of righteousness flows through me and I am victorious in Christ!

April 28

If any of you is deficient in wisdom, let him ask of the giving God (Who gives) to every one liberally and ungrudgingly, without reproaching or faultfinding, and it will be given him. Only it must be in faith that he asks, with no wavering—no hesitating, no doubting. For the one who wavers (hesitates, doubts) is like the billowing surge out at sea, that is blown hither and thither and tossed by the wind (James 1:5, 6 Amp.).

Father, I just thank you for all the things I can ask in the name of Jesus. Thank you for telling me that if I lack wisdom, all I have to do is ask and it is mine, given liberally without question. I rejoice in the strength of faith I have to ask and receive from you, and I thank you that I'm not blown this way and that way like a weathervane. Thank you, Father, that my faith is steady and constant. I really appreciate the fact that, even though I might be very deficient in natural wisdom, because I have asked, I have received divine wisdom. Thank you for giving me the mind of Christ.

April 29

Submit yourselves therefore to God. Resist the devil, and he will flee from you. Draw nigh to God, and he will draw nigh to you. Cleanse your hands, ye sinners; and purify your hearts, ye double minded (James 4:7, 8).

Devil, I'm resisting you, so you can't come close to me. Thank you, Father, that I can come before you with clean hands and a pure heart. I submit myself completely to you, giving thanks that as I draw near to you, you come closer and closer to me. I praise you, Father, that I have power not only to resist the devil, but to chase him away completely. He *has to flee* before your power. No longer will I be double-minded, with wavering and divided interests; but I shall be single-minded, desiring only to serve and love you. The devil can't touch me.

April 30

For if thou altogether holdest thy peace at this time, then shall there enlargement and deliverance arise to the Jews from another place; but thou and thy father's house shall be destroyed: and who knoweth whether thou art come to the kingdom for such a time as this? (Esther 4:14).

Father, how we bless you that Jesus came to the world for such a time as this. Thank you that your timing is perfect in all things. We are excited about that day when your perfect timing will close the world as we know it today and the book will be completed. We know it will be just at the right time. In the midst of the world's failing economic system, thank you that we stand on that solid rock—Jesus. We glory in your perfect timing.

May

BLESSINGS

God Wants You to Be Blessed

God loves us so much that his heart cries when we don't avail ourselves of all the blessings he wants to give us. Look how easy he makes it for us: *Christ hath redeemed us from the curse of the law, being made a curse for us: for it is written, Cursed is everyone that hangeth on a tree,* ***that the blessing of Abraham might come on the Gentiles, through Jesus Christ*** *. . . and if ye be Christ's, then are ye Abraham's seed, and heirs according to the promise* (Galatians 3:13, 14, 29). Every blessing that belonged to Abraham belongs to you and me. Hallelujah!

We are what we say. So many times we confess what the devil's book of lies says instead of what the Word of God says. Sometimes it's a real blessing to read what you can expect from God after you have fulfilled the things he wants you to do. I especially love the way Moses talks about these blessings in Deuteronomy, Chapter 28, in the Amplified Bible.

If you will listen diligently to the voice of the Lord your God, being watchful to do all His commandments which I command you this day, the Lord your God will set you high above all the nations of the earth, and all these blessings shall come upon you and overtake you, if you heed the voice of the Lord your God. There it is! I love the way God wrote the conditions; they are so simple and easy to understand. All we have to do is to listen to his voice. How do we do that? By reading his Word. What does it say to do next? It tells us to make sure that we do *all* the things he tells us to do. He doesn't want us going around doing our own thing; he wants us to do what his Word says.

If you want to have all the blessings God has for you, just listen to *him*, and *don't* listen to the temptations the devil tries to put on you in thought, deed, and word. Now look at what God has for you.

BLESSED *shall you be in the city, and* ***BLESSED*** *shall you be in the field.* ***BLESSED*** *shall be the fruit of your body, and the fruit of your ground, and the fruit of your beasts, the increase of cattle, and the young of your flock.*

BLESSED *shall be your basket and your kneading trough.* (That means you're not going to have to worry when bread gets to be $20 a loaf and roast beef $43.69 per pound, because your basket is blessed. Hallelujah!)

BLESSED *shall you be when you come in, and* ***BLESSED*** *shall you be when you go out.*

The Lord shall cause your enemies who rise up against you to be defeated before your face; they shall come out against you one way, and flee before you seven ways. The Lord shall command the ***BLESSINGS*** *upon you in your storehouse, and* ***in all that you undertake;*** *and He will* ***BLESS*** *you in the land which the Lord your God gives you.* (Wow, every single thing that I do is going to be blessed.)

The Lord will establish you as a people holy to Himself, as He has sworn to you. ***If you keep the commandments of the Lord your God, and walk in his ways.*** [Not in the devil's ways, but in God's ways.] . . . *And the Lord shall make you have a surplus of prosperity* [I receive that, Lord], . . . *The Lord shall open to you His good treasury* [Thank you, Father, because you own everything there is, so I have access to everything there is, just because you're opening up to me your good treasury], . . . *and the Lord shall make you the head, and not the tail.* (I'm so glad I do the wagging, instead of being wagged, aren't you?)

The verses above are from the first thirteen verses of Chapter 28 of Deuteronomy. They should be read every day until expecting the blessings of God becomes an actual part of our being.

Remember, you can't walk with the devil and have the promises of God. This is why many people wonder why they're not blessed. They want God's blessings, but they also want to do what they want to do, and the two just don't go together. You can't walk on two sides of the street at the same time.

When you walk outside the will of God, he really has a lot to say about what's going to happen to you. Listen to what he says starting with the fifteenth verse of Deuteronomy, Chapter 28. Remember, he has just finished telling us about all the blessings that belong to us if we obey him, but *If you will not obey the voice of the Lord your God, being watchful to do all His commandments and His statutes which I command you this day, then all these* ***curses*** *shall come upon you and overtake you.* ***Cursed*** *shall you be in the city, and* ***cursed*** *shall you be in the field.* ***Cursed*** *shall be your basket and your kneading trough* [watch out for those high prices]. ***Cursed*** *shall be the fruit of your body, of your land, of the increase of your cattle and the young of your sheep.* ***Cursed*** *shall you be when you come in, and* ***cursed*** *shall you be when you go out. The Lord shall send you* ***curses****, confusion, and rebuke in every enterprise to which you set your hand, until you are destroyed, perishing quickly, because of the evil of your doings, by which you have forsaken me. The Lord will make the pestilence cling to you until He has consumed you from off the land, which you go to possess. The Lord will smite you with consumption, with fever, and inflammation, fiery heat, sword and drought, blasting, and mildew; they shall pursue you until you perish* (Deuteronomy 28:15-22 Amp.).

Wow, who in their right mind would ever choose what is promised to us when we follow the devil? Don't you praise God that we have chosen to walk with Jesus and to walk in his blessings? I'd certainly hate to think of having all those curses laid down upon me. Yet there are people who just think they have to give up so much. You give up all the blessings of God when you follow the devil. Hallelujah, I'm so glad we're on the winning side, aren't you?

God's blessings are just waiting up there in a big storehouse for us to claim them. God loves even the worst sinner so much that he wants even that one who is lost to come under his blessings. Let's share with people about the blessings of God, so they'll want the same thing. They'll never know how real it is *until they see it in your life.*

Then the greatest blessing of all follows: God gets blessed when we accept his blessings. The giver always gets blessed more than the receiver.

May 1

Blessed is the man that walketh not in the counsel of the ungodly, nor standeth in the way of sinners, nor sitteth in the seat of the scornful. But his delight is in the law of the Lord; and in his law doth he meditate day and night. And he shall be like a tree planted by the rivers of water, that bringeth forth his fruit in his season; his leaf also shall not wither; and whatsoever he doeth shall prosper (Psalm 1:1-3).

Father, I'm blessed, blessed, blessed. I'm happy, fortunate, and prosperous, because I don't follow the advice, plans, or purposes of the ungodly. I'm blessed because I'm not inactive where sinners are concerned. Just lead me to them, and I'll share the Good News. I certainly am not going to sit down with the scoffers and mockers, but I constantly meditate in your laws and your words. I bless you that your promises are music to my ears and sweet as honey in my mouth. I thank you that everything I do in you prospers in a marvelous way, because my joy is in your law.

May 2

The Lord is my shepherd; I shall not want. He maketh me to lie down in green pastures: he leadeth me beside the still waters. He restoreth my soul: he leadeth me in the paths of righteousness for his name's sake (Psalm 23:1-3).

I lack nothing in my life, Father, because you lead me to beautiful places where I am nourished and at peace, both physically and spiritually. Father, I praise you and thank you for that, because you are my Shepherd, my light, and my hope. You feed and clothe me and restore my soul when I'm weary, because you love me as a shepherd loves his flock. I thank you that, whenever I'm rushing around too much, you lead me beside the still waters, out of the turmoil of life. Thank you, Father, for protecting me from the wolves of the world and for leading me in the paths of righteousness.

May 3

Yea, though I walk through the valley of the shadow of death, I will fear no evil: for thou art with me; thy rod and thy staff they comfort me. Thou preparest a table before me in the presence of mine enemies (Psalm 23:4, 5).

Father, Thank you that I don't walk into the valley of the shadow of death and sit down. No, you've said that I walk *through* the deep, sunless valley of the shadow of death. Hallelujah, I'm walking right out of that valley, whether it be sickness, poverty, or depression, and I fear or dread no evil, because *you* protect me. Thank you for preparing a spiritual feast for me right in front of my enemies. I don't even have to ask them to sit down, because they don't have any right to disturb me. They turn their back on spiritual food anyway; but, hallelujah, it cures *my* indigestion!

May 4

Thou anointest my head with oil; my cup runneth over. Surely goodness and mercy shall follow me all the days of my life: and I will dwell in the house of the Lord for ever (Psalm 23:5, 6).

How I rejoice, Father, that I'm so blessed, because you anoint my head with so much of the oil of the Holy Spirit that my cup runs over. You didn't give me just a little trickle, you gave me a cup that runs and runs and runs over. Thank you, Father, that two things are going to follow me all the days of my life—goodness and mercy. Not sorrow and sadness, but goodness and mercy. I thank you because I'm blessed to be able to dwell in the house of the Lord forever.

May 5

Blessed is he whose transgression is forgiven, whose sin is covered (Psalm 32:1).

I'm blessed. I'm happy. I'm fortunate. I'm to be envied. All because my sins are forgiven. My sins are covered by that precious blood in such a way that you can't even see them. I'm walking on air, because a huge burden—all my sins—has been lifted from my shoulders and replaced by that wonderful blessing—a covering of Jesus's blood. I'm walking on air. How I bless you that the blood of Jesus was sufficient to cover the sins of the whole world, including mine, and I praise you that when you forgive sins you also forget them. I'm a brand-new person to you! How I bless you because of the tremendous and unending supply of love you've poured out on me.

May 6

Delight thyself also in the Lord; and he shall give thee the desires of thine heart. Commit thy way unto the Lord; trust also in him; and he shall bring it to pass (Psalm 37:4, 5).

I delighted in you and with you, Lord, and my heart is overflowing with good measure. You see deep into my heart, and you give me the desires of my heart first of all, because you have taken out those carnal desires of the flesh I once had and have replaced them with your divine desires. You even grant those secret requests that no one knows about except you and me. How I praise you because, since I've committed my life to you and trust you completely, you will give me what I desire—the real grade

"A" things and no grade "B" substitutes or plastic imitations. No one has a better father than I do, because *you* are my Father, and your promises stagger my wildest imagination. Hallelujah! I'm blessed because you're bringing things to pass. Glory!

May 7

Read all of Psalm 136 before making the following confession.

Heavenly Father, I'm blessed because you are a good God and your mercy endures forever. I've committed sins that seemed to be unforgivable, but in your mercy you have forgiven them. You've given me a beautiful world in which to live because of your mercy. You have given me friends who delight my heart, and you've kept my enemies off my back, because of your mercy. Lord, You didn't have to do any of these things for me—but you did because of your mercy. Thank you, Father, for your loving-kindness and mercy, which are not temporary things, but eternal, everlasting blessings. They continue unceasingly and eternally. They never wear out or go sour, but they last forever and forever.

May 8

Thou has beset me behind and before, and laid thine hand upon me. Such knowledge is too wonderful for me; it is high, I cannot attain unto it. Whither shall I go from thy spirit? or whither shall I flee from thy presence? If I ascend up into heaven, thou art there: if I make my bed in hell, behold thou art there. If I take the wings of the morning, and dwell in the uttermost parts of the sea; Even there shall thy hand lead me, and thy right hand shall hold me (Psalm 139:5-10).

Father, I'm blessed by your glorious presence wherever I go, whether I'm in Arkansas, New York, Zambia, or China. If I were an astronaut, Father, I'd find you in outer space. I rejoice in the blessing of your presence, from which I never want to depart, for it's your hand that guides me along the straight and narrow path. Thank you, Lord, for your presence in my life. Thank you that I can never be lost to your sight.

May 9

Blessed be the Lord my strength, which teacheth my hands to war, and my fingers to fight: My goodness, and my fortress; my high tower, and my deliverer; my shield, and he in whom I trust; who subdueth my people under me (Psalm 144:1, 2).

Father, I'm blessed because your keen strength and supreme power protect me under all conditions, no matter how difficult they look. I'm blessed too because your strength makes me a spiritual warrior, armed with the razor-sharp sword of your righteousness, so that I actively take part in the war against darkness. I'm blessed because you never leave me or forsake me and because your steadfast love surrounds me at all times. You are my high tower of safety, my deliverer, and my shield to protect me from the darts of the devil at all times, and you subdue those enemies who try to attack me. I glory in such a glorious God.

May 10

Blessed be the God and Father of our Lord Jesus Christ, who hath blessed us with all spiritual blessings in heavenly places in Christ (Ephesians 1:3).

All spiritual blessings in heavenly places are mine. I give you praise, laudation, and eulogy, because you are the Father of our Lord Jesus Christ, the Messiah. I rejoice that Jesus is with you in heaven and is preparing a place for me there, because I'm ready for that wonderful day when he will come to get me and take me home to you. In the meantime, I'm going to enjoy all those Holy Spirit–given blessings in heaven and earth, which you've passed on to us through your wonderful Son. Glory!

May 11

Christ hath redeemed us from the curse of the law, being made a curse for us: for it is written, Cursed is everyone that hangeth on a tree: That the blessing of Abraham might come on the Gentiles through Jesus Christ; that we might receive the promise of the Spirit through faith . . . And if ye be Christ's, then are ye Abraham's seed, and heirs according to the promise (Galatians 3:13, 14, 29).

I'm redeemed by the blood of the Lamb. I'm free from the curse. Father, I'm so blessed that I've been redeemed from the curse of the law by Jesus Christ, who was made a curse for me, so that the blessings of Abraham might come to me. I thank you for sending the Lord Jesus to wash my sins away and remove the curse that separated me from you and your love. Your love lifts and blesses me constantly. Thank you, Father, for your endless blessings. Bless you for making me an heir to all the promises of Abraham, because I am his seed.

May 12

But be not deceived; God is not mocked: for whatsoever a man soweth, that shall he also reap. For he that soweth to his flesh shall of the flesh reap corruption; but he that soweth to the Spirit shall of the Spirit reap life everlasting (Galatians 6:7, 8).

I'm overcome with blessings today, Father, because you've promised that whatever we sow, we shall reap. I'm sowing a bumper crop of love, joy, and peace today, Father. I'm not planting my seed in the unfertile soil of the flesh, because I don't want to reap corruption. I'm sowing to the Spirit to be able to reap life everlasting. I praise you that my life is not down here, but my real life is in heaven with you and Jesus. I'm blessed because you make this all possible for me personally, and how I love you for this.

May 13

And hath raised us up together, and made us sit together in heavenly places in Christ Jesus: That in the ages to come he might shew the exceeding riches of his grace in his kindness toward us through Christ Jesus. For by grace are ye saved through faith; and that not of yourselves: it is the gift of God: Not of works, lest any man should boast (Ephesians 2:6-9).

Glory to God, you've raised me up, and I'm sitting in heavenly places in Christ Jesus. I love you for that. Thank you, Father, that my salvation is not dependent upon my good works but is entirely dependent upon your grace. You so simply said that if I would believe in Jesus Christ, his work at Calvary, and his blood, and if I would confess it with my mouth, that I would be saved. Hallelujah, Father, I'm saved and filled with your love. I can't boast about it either, because you did it all.

May 14

That Christ may dwell in your hearts by faith; that ye, being rooted and grounded in love, May be able to comprehend with all saints what is the breadth, and length, and depth, and height; And to know the love of Christ, which passeth knowledge, that ye might be filled with all the fulness of God (Ephesians 3:17, 19).

Thank you, Father, for blessing me with the knowledge that Christ lives in my heart, because I trust in him. I thank you for blessing me so much with that tremendous love, which is so long, so wide, so high, and so deep that I will never really be able to understand the greatness of it. Thank you, Father, for the knowledge that some beautiful day I will be filled all the way up to the top with you. What a promise. I don't deserve it, but I receive it.

May 15

Finally, my brethren, be strong in the Lord, and in the power of his might. Put on the whole armour of God, that ye may be able to stand against the wiles of the devil (Ephesians 6:10, 11). (*Read also* Ephesians 6:12-17.)

I praise you, Father, for blessing me with your strength and with the power of your might. Because *you* provided my whole armor, it is invincible, inconquerable, unyielding, and indomitable. I am blessed because, even though I don't wrestle against flesh and blood, but against principalities, against powers, against the rulers of the darkness of this world, and against spiritual wickedness in high places, you have given me your whole armor to wear for protection. With the power of your might going before me, Father, I will *always* be victorious.

May 16

Blessed be the Lord, that hath given rest unto his people Israel, according to all that he promised: there hath not failed one word of all his good promise (I Kings 8:56).

What a blessing it is to serve you, Father, because when the world lies and cheats and fails to keep its word, you are always right there, fulfilling all your promises. Thank you that the God of Abraham, Isaac, and Jacob knows my name too. Thank you for being a God of integrity, Father, so that we can be imitators of you and be people of integrity in all our dealings. Thank you that all the blessings of Abraham are mine. Your Word promises this, and you never fail to keep your promises. Hallelujah, what a God I serve. I'm blessed.

May 17

And God blessed them, and God said unto them, Be fruitful, and multiply, and replenish the earth, and subdue it: and have dominion over the fish of the sea, and over the fowl of the air, and over every living thing that moveth upon the earth (Genesis 1:28).

Father, I'm being overtaken and overcome with blessings again because of your love. I'm blessed, I'm blessed, I'm blessed because I have dominion over the fish of the sea, over the fowl of the air, and over all living things. I'm blessed because I can be used to multiply your family. I'm blessed because I am fruitful. I'm blessed because I was made in your likeness. I'm blessed because this blessing was upon both man and woman alike, in whom there is no difference in your sight. Glory!

May 18

Arise, walk through the land in the length of it and in the breadth of it; for I will give it unto thee (Genesis 13:17).

Father, what blessings you give us. Thank you for the privilege of knowing that all the blessings you bestowed in the beginning have come right down through time to us. Thank you for letting us walk through the length and breadth of the land you have for us, knowing that you will give it to us. Thank you for blessing those who bless me and who confer prosperity or happiness upon me. Thank you that I can also be a blessing to others by dispensing good to them. Thank you for giving me so much land (or possessions) that I have too much and can share them with others. How I bless you for all your blessings. I'm walking sideways, forward, and backward over the land you give to me.

May 19

Jesus Christ the same yesterday, and today, and for ever (Hebrews 13:8).

Father, I praise and thank you that your Son alone, among all the constant changes taking place in the world, always remains the same. I thank you that because of this he still saves, heals, and delivers. He is the living cornerstone of my life, and I am saved, healed, and delivered, because he hasn't changed one single bit and never will. I thank you that when the price of gold escalates and soars to new highs and drops to new lows, Jesus never changes. Thank you for blessing me with a changeless Jesus as my Savior; my Healer; my doorway into your marvelous, glorious presence. He is my rock, and I can rely on his sameness forever.

May 20

Be patient therefore, brethren, unto the coming of the Lord. Behold, the husbandman waiteth for the precious fruit of the earth, and hath long patience for it, until he receives the early and latter rain (James 5:7).

Heavenly Father, thank you for the blessed hope I have in the coming of my Lord Jesus Christ. I'm blessed now, Father, because he lives in my heart, waiting for exactly the chosen day to come to me in person. Thank you for your Word, Father, which tells me that Christ is like the farmer who waits for the seasonal rains to bring his crop to full ripeness before the harvest time. I praise you, Father, for patiently perfecting me in your love, so I'll be joyously prepared for that great day. Hallelujah!

May 21

Being born again, not of corruptible seed, but of incorruptible, by the word of God, which liveth and abideth for ever. For all flesh is as grass, and all the glory of man as the flower of the grass. The grass withereth, and the flower thereof falleth away: But the word of the Lord endureth for ever. And this is the word which by the gospel is preached unto you (I Peter 1:23-25).

Glory, Father, I'm born again and glad of it. The incorruptible seed of your Word has been planted in my heart and is growing every day. I praise you, Father, that, although the things of this world come and go, your Word endures forever, a priceless, eternal treasure. Thank you for the blessing of your Word. You are not temporary; you are eternal and everlasting, never wearing out.

May 22

For God so loved the world, that he gave his only begotten Son, that whosoever believeth in him should not perish, but have everlasting life (John 3:16).

Thank you, Father, that because of your love I can answer my telephone and say, "God loves you!" and feel your love going right through that telephone to the person on the other end. Thank you, Father, that you love us so much. It's this love that makes your blessings available to us. Thank you that I am blessed, because you loved me enough to send your only begotten Son, Jesus, to die for me, so that I might have eternal life. I love you, Father. I believe, I believe, I believe.

May 23

But ye are a chosen generation, a royal priesthood, an holy nation, a peculiar people; that ye should show forth the praises of him who hath called you out of darkness into his marvelous light (I Peter 2:9).

I'm glad I'm different and unique. I'm blessed to belong to a chosen race, a royal priesthood, a dedicated nation and to be a member of your own purchased, special people. Thank you that I can set forth and show to all the world your wonderful deeds and display the virtues and perfections of your divine nature, because you have implanted it in me to minister to the spiritual needs of those around me. I rejoice that I belong to this peculiar race of people and that my Lord is King of kings and Lord of lords. He has the power to call whosoever he will out of darkness and death into the marvelous light of new life. Thank you, Father, for giving me the blessing of Jesus and your love in Him. I'm peculiar, and I want the world to know the reason for it. Hallelujah!

May 24

For the eyes of the Lord are over the righteous, and his ears are open unto their prayers: but the face of the Lord is against them that do evil (I Peter 3:12).

Hallelujah, I can't hide from you, Father. I'm so blessed that your eyes are upon the righteous, those who are in right standing with you, because your Word says that you are attentive and sensitive to my prayers. I'm blessed because your ears are open to me twenty-four hours a day. How I praise you for never tiring of listening to me. Thank you that I am never lost to your sight, but I am under your tender, loving care at all times. How I praise you that you differentiate between the evil and the righteous, because I would never want to have you turn your face from me. I'm never going to even try to hide from you.

May 25

And whatsoever we ask, we receive of him, because we keep his commandments, and do those things that are pleasing in his sight (I John 3:22).

Whatsoever I ask is mine. Glory, what a promise, Father. I'm blessed because you've given me instructions for life that are written down in a book that I can constantly refer to. Because you shower me with so much love, I rejoice to obey everything you tell me to do. You bless me with your faithfulness, so I bless you with mine. I watchfully and carefully obey all your instructions and do the things that are pleasing in your sight. I observe your suggestions and constantly practice what is pleasing to you, so I thank you for being willing to do whatsoever I ask, because my wishes are in line with what you want for me! Glory, I'm swimming in blessings.

May 26

There is no fear in love; but perfect love casteth out fear: because fear hath torment. He that feareth is not made perfect in love (I John 4:18).

Father, I'm blessed that I have no fear in me whatsoever, because I'm protected by your power and strength from all the things of the devil. By your Word, I have no fear in me, and dread does not exist, because your full-blown, perfect love turns fear out-of-doors and gets rid of every trace of terror. I'm blessed, Father, and I praise you that

I'm not suffering the torment of darkness, because you've lifted me into the wonderful light and complete perfection of your love. Thank you, Father, for blessing me. Regardless of the circumstances, your love overcomes *all* fear.

May 27

Are they not all ministering spirits, sent forth to minister for them who shall be heirs of salvation? (Hebrews 1:14).

Thank you, Father, for sending out your angels, who are ministering for us constantly, because we are heirs of salvation. Thank you, Father, for blessing us with the knowledge that those same angels are out there bringing our loved ones to that person who will minister salvation to them. Thank you that you send angels forth even without my knowing about it, except believing they are there. Thank you for letting them minister for my protection in times of trouble. Thank you that they keep my foot from slipping when the path gets dangerous. Thank you that they could even pet a lion and close his mouth without danger to a child of God. I'm blessed because of angels.

May 28

That the God of our Lord Jesus Christ, the Father of glory, may give unto you the spirit of wisdom and revelation in the knowledge of him: The eyes of your understanding being enlightened; that ye may know what is the hope of his calling, and what the riches of the glory of his inheritance in the saints (Ephesians 1:17, 18).

Glory, Father, your blessings are overwhelming me with joy, because you have granted me a spirit of wisdom, revelation, and insight into mysteries and secrets in the deep and intimate knowledge of your Son. I thank you because you have flooded the eyes of my heart with light, giving me the privilege of understanding what is the hope of my calling and the riches that are the glorious inheritance of your set-apart ones. I'm blessed because of the magnitude of your blessings.

May 29

For ye know the grace of our Lord Jesus Christ, that, though he was rich, yet for your sakes he became poor, that ye through his poverty might be rich (II Corinthians 8:9).

Father, your blessings stagger my imagination. When I consider that Jesus had everything in your Kingdom, with all its riches and glories for himself, yet he chose to become poor for my sake, that I could become rich in you, I am overwhelmed. I praise you that I have been delivered from the curse through him. I bless you that I am saved through grace, because there is no way I could have earned the gift Jesus gave me. It was his kindness and his gracious generosity that make this all possible. I thank you that because of his poverty, I have become enriched and abundantly supplied at all times. I thank you that I am progressively becoming acquainted with these blessings more and more all the time.

May 30

While we look not at the things which are seen, but at the things which are not seen: for the things which are seen are temporal; but the things which are not seen are eternal (II Corinthians 4:18).

Thank you, Father, for giving me spiritual eyes so that I don't have to look and see things the way the world sees them, but I can look at them through your eyes. Thank you that I don't have to see only the things that are visible to our human eyes, but I can see with my spiritual eyes the glorious things of your Kingdom, which is my inheritance. I praise you for this great blessing. I bless you because, even though I've never seen you, I *know* you're there at all times, loving and protecting me.

May 31

Don't let others spoil your faith and joy with their philosophies, their wrong and shallow answers built on men's thoughts and ideas, instead of on what Christ has said, For in Christ there is all of God in a human body; so you have everything when you have Christ, and you are filled with God through your union with Christ. He is the highest Ruler, with authority over every other power (Colossians 2:8, 9 LB).

I have everything! Father, what an overwhelming thought to know that I am in Christ and he is in me. All the treasures of divine wisdom and all the riches of spiritual knowledge and enlightenment are stored up and lie hidden in him. But they are mine, and I have everything, because I am joined with Jesus Christ in salvation. Father, the world can't talk me out of what your Word says is mine. My joy and my faith are at an all-time high, because they stand on what Christ has said. I don't look to the world for its shallow answers and intellectualism, but I look to the Holy Spirit for my answers to life. Bless you, Father, that you tell us with no qualms that Jesus is the highest Ruler. Not only that, he is mine. Hallelujah, therefore I have everything I need in Christ Jesus!

June

LOVE

Love is our devotion subject for the month of June, and what an appropriate subject for the month when people think of love and marriage. The love of God for man and of man for God, is the most beautiful love in all the world, because it is this love that makes us lovable to the world and makes it possible for us to love them. God loves to hear you tell him how much you love him, so say it every day, will you?

In the devotion for June 11, we have asked you to pick out someone to love in a special way. Write and tell us what happened to you and to the person because of this special day of giving love.

If you want to see some problems you have disappear in a hurry, write all the problems on a piece of paper, and at the bottom write: *In ALL these things we are more than conquerors through him that loved us* (Romans 8:37). Confess it every day until you discover that *every single one of those problems is conquered.*

June 1

As the Father hath loved me, so have I loved you: continue ye in my love. If ye keep my commandments, ye shall abide in my love; even as I have kept my Father's commandments, and abide in his love. These things have I spoken unto you, that my joy might remain in you, and that your joy might be full (John 15:9-11).

My joy is running over and spilling all over the place. Thank you, Father, that in the same way you loved Jesus, he has also loved me. Thank you, Jesus, that because I keep your commandments, I abide in your love all the time. I thank you that I can abide in your love twenty-four hours a day, because your source never runs out and is always available to me. Thank you that my joy is full and running over. Thank you that you gave your joy, not as a temporary thing, but as a permanent, full-time gift, so that your joy, happiness, and excitement remain in me and are full, complete, and overflowing at all times.

June 2

Jesus answered and said unto him, If a man love me, he will keep my words: and my Father will love him, and we will come unto him, and make our abode with him (John 14:23).

Jesus, I love you, I love you, I love you. Father, thank you that your Son is so lovable. Thank you that I can love him at all times and keep his words, because his words are true and right and holy. Thank you, Jesus, for giving me words that last forever and never change. How I praise you, because you have come to live in me and make your abode in me. Because your love fills me to overflowing, I can love others, not just neighbors, but even enemies. I love you for being so close to me at all times. I thank you that your house is my house and my house is your house.

June 3

But as it is written, Eye hath not seen, nor ear heard, neither have entered into the heart of man, the things which God hath prepared for them that love him (I Corinthians 2:9).

I'm excited today, because I can hardly wait to hear what you're telling me. I praise you, Father, that whether or not I have 20/20 vision, my eyes have not seen, nor are they capable of seeing, all the love that you have for me. Thank you that, regardless of how good my hearing is, my ears will never be able to hear all the wonderful truths that you have ready for me. My heart belongs to you, Father, and I'm rejoicing right now because I know you'll have something beautiful beyond words to put in it. Thank you that all these wonderful gifts are especially for me, because you love me.

June 4

But God commendeth his love toward us, in that, while we were yet sinners, Christ died for us (Romans 5:8).

I was the worst of them all, and yet you still loved me. Thank you, Father, that you loved me in spite of what I was. You didn't look at my faults and failures, but you looked at what you wanted to see in me. How I praise you, Father, that you let your Son die. Your love for me was so great that you were willing to let his blood be shed to save me. I receive your love and enjoy it every day, because I remember what that love was willing to do. It thrills me when I realize that I didn't have to clean myself up in order to have Jesus willing to die for me; he was willing to do it when I was a miserable character.

June 5

Nevertheless the Lord thy God would not hearken unto Balaam; but the Lord thy God turned the curse into a blessing unto thee, because the Lord thy God loved thee (Deuteronomy 23:5).

Father, how I praise you that you wouldn't listen to Balaam, even when he was willing to curse Israel for money. You loved your people so much that you were willing to turn the curse into a blessing each time he opened his mouth. Thank you, Father, that the love that reached your people back in the Old Testament times still reaches me today. I love you for this, Father. I thank you that when my mouth gets out of line, Father, and begins to say the wrong things that don't glorify you, you can still turn my words around to be a blessing to others.

June 6

He that hath my commandments, and keepeth them, he it is that loveth me: and he that loveth me shall be loved of my Father, and I will love him, and will manifest myself to him (John 14:21).

I praise you, Father, that Jesus has given us commandments to keep. These commandments make the Christian life so simple and straightforward to live; all we have to do is what you tell us to do and refrain from doing the things you tell us not to do. Thus we're blessed and living in your love right now. How we praise you, Jesus, that you have promised to manifest yourself to us, because we love you. You've said that you will let yourself be clearly seen and make yourself real to me at all times. I really love you.

June 7

He that loveth not knoweth not God; for God is love (I John 4:8).

Father, thank you that your Word tells me the greatest commandment is to love you with every fiber of my being, and the second is to love my neighbor as myself. I obey these commandments so that you will live in my heart and fill me up with even more love. I praise you because, when you created me, you made me able to receive and to give love. You *are* love, and the river of your love flows continually to your people. I rejoice in your love, Father, and I thank you for letting us know in no uncertain terms that there is plenty of love for all those who open their hearts to receive it. I love you, Father.

June 8

Beloved, if God so loved us, we ought also to love one another (I John 4:11).

Thank you, Father, for showing us that you love us so much that there just isn't any excuse for us not loving one another. Thank you for giving me a soft heart and the ability to love all my brothers and sisters on this earth. I know I could never do this on my own, but it's so wonderful to know that, because you could love me through all my sin, all my faults, and all my failures, you can give me the ability to love even those people who seem unlovable. Thank you, Father, for your Word, which teaches that everybody deserves love.

June 9

And we have known and believed the love that God hath to us. God is love; and he that dwelleth in love dwelleth in God, and God in him (I John 4:16).

I glorify your name, Father, because I know and believe how much you love me. You washed my sin away with the blood of Jesus, and there just isn't any way I can imagine a greater love than that. There isn't any way I can thank you enough for what you did. But, Father, I want to try—by loving you with everything I've got and by obeying you in all things. I thank you, Father, that I dwell in love because of your love for me, and because of the power of your love, I live in you and you live in me.

June 10

This is my commandment, That ye love one another, as I have loved you. Greater love hath no man than this, that a man lay down his life for his friends (John 15:12, 13).

Love is the greatest force in the world, Lord Jesus, and the most powerful word in the Bible except *God* and *Christ Jesus.* I thank you for commanding me to love others in the same way that you love me. I am thankful that you not only gave your life for your friends, but you gave it for me, even though I was an enemy for so many years. How I praise you for showing me the way to love others. I will express your love in me to those I meet, even to those who are hard to love.

June 11

And thou shalt love the Lord thy God with all thy heart, and with all thy soul, and with all thy mind, and with all thy strength: this is the first commandment (Mark 12:30).

Father, I love you with all my mind, my heart, my strength, and my soul. Because you love me so much, it's easy to love you in return. I worship you, Father, because your first commandment concerns love, which is what everyone in the world needs and deserves. Thank you that in loving you, I receive the power to love everyone. I will find a specific individual to love today. I will concentrate on finding a person who needs love, someone who does not have many friends and whose heart is crying out for love. I'm going to love that person today with your special love.

June 12

A new commandment I give unto you, That ye love one another; as I have loved you, that ye also love one another (John 13:34).

Thank you, Father, that Jesus gave us a new commandment. I praise you that people know we are his disciples because we love in a new way—we love one another *as he loved us*. Thank you that Jesus loved us enough to teach us, heal us, and save us from sin by even dying for us. Thank you that this is your limitless love flowing through me right now, a powerful love that enables me to love everyone even as Jesus did. Thank you, Father, that when I obey this commandment to love others, I am at the same time loving you with all my heart, my soul, my mind, and my strength.

June 13

And I pray that Christ will be more and more at home in your hearts, living within you as you trust in him. May your roots go down deep into the soil of God's marvelous love; and may you be able to feel and understand, as all God's children should, how long, how wide, how deep, and how high his love really is; and to experience this love for yourselves, though it is so great that you will never see the end of it or fully know or understand it. And so at last you will be filled up with God himself (Ephesians 3:17-19 LB).

Jesus, be more and more at home in my heart. Father, I praise you that Jesus lives in me. Thank you that my roots are going all the way down, deep into your soil, which enables me to feel the tremendous depth of your love for me, even though I know I will never be able to comprehend it with my limited mind. Father, I'm so excited, because you promise that some day I will be filled all the way up to the top with you. Glory!

June 14

I have given them the glory you gave me—the glorious unity of being one, as we are—I in them and you in me, all being perfected into one—so that the world will know you sent me and will understand that you love them as much as you love me (John 17:22, 23 LB).

Father, I love you, I love you, I love you for so many different reasons but especially for the glorious perfect unity we have in Christ Jesus. He lives in us, you live in him, and we're all perfected into one glorious body. Father, how you could ever love me as much as you love Jesus is beyond my human comprehension, but I praise you that you do love me just as much as you do Jesus.

June 15

And Ruth said, Entreat me not to leave thee, or to return from following after thee: for whither thou goest, I will go; and where thou lodgest, I will lodge: thy people shall *by my people, and thy God my God: Where thou diest, will I die, and there will I be buried: the Lord do so to me, and more also, if ought but death part thee and me* (Ruth 1:16, 17).

Thank you, Father, that this can apply to marriage, and thank you for giving to each married couple the most beautiful words to say to each other that can be said. How we bless you, Father, for encouraging us to stay together in marriage at all times. Thank you for the sacredness of human love as well as divine love, and for allowing us to love our mates in greater ways because of your love pouring through us. I bless you that my place is beside my mate at all times. Bless you for making these words available to all.

June 16

There is no fear in love; but perfect love casteth out fear: because fear hath torment. He that feareth is not made perfect in love (I John 4:18).

Thank you, Father, that your perfect, complete, full-grown, faultless love turns fear out-of-doors and gets rid of every trace of terror. I glory in the knowledge that the devil can't touch me with fear, because your love is so complete and surrounds me like a glove and safely wraps me in a love cocoon. I praise you, Father, for letting us grow into love's complete perfection because of your great love for us. Thank you for a love that is without a blemish and unparalleled in human understanding, but which is mine because I belong to you. I love you, Father.

June 17

He that loveth father or mother more than me is not worthy of me: and he that loveth son or daughter more than me is not worthy of me (Matthew 10:37).

Father, I love you more than anything in the whole, wide world. I praise you, Father, because you command and demand that we love you more than our mother, father, or even our children. Thank you for always knowing what is best for us, because in giving you first place in our lives and loving you most, you've given us the opportunity to love our own families even more because of your love flowing through us. Thank you for giving me the desire and the ability to love you more than my family and to cling steadfastly to you and walk in your ways. Bless you, Father, because the love of my family is based on you and not on my own desires. You have first place in my heart.

June 18

Walk in love, as Christ also hath loved us, and hath given himself for us an offering and a sacrifice to God for a sweetsmelling savour (Ephesians 5:2).

Father, I'm walking in love. I'm running in love. I'm leaping in love. I'm falling in love with Jesus. Thank you for loving us so much and giving us someone so lovable. I'm walking down streets with love, letting it ooze out over the people who don't even like me. I'm talking in love to everyone I meet, including those who try to gyp me! I'm thinking in love, even when my thoughts might be trying to go in other directions. I'm a lover, because you've put love into my heart.

June 19

Her sins, which are many, are forgiven; for she loved much: but to whom little is forgiven, the same loveth little (Luke 7:47).

Father, thank you that I can say like Paul that I was the worst of sinners, and because you forgave so much, it's so easy for me to love you wholeheartedly, without any reservations whatsoever. I love you, Father, because you didn't have just a little to forgive in me, you had a lot; but I thank you that you forgave everything you might have ever held against me, so I love you much, much, much. I bless you because as a result of your forgiveness I walk in peace and in freedom from all the problems that are the result of sin. No wonder I love you so much!

June 20

Don't be teamed with those who do not love the Lord, for what do the people of God have in common with the people of sin? How can light live with darkness? (II Corinthians 6:14 LB).

Lord, I love you so much because you tell us exactly how to find favor in your eyes. Thank you for telling us that we're not to team up with people who don't love you, because that inner being of ours tells us that we don't have anything in common with them. We praise you that you say so simply and effectively that, just as darkness and light don't go together, neither do God and sin. Thank you, Lord, that we walk in the light. Thank you for saving us from mismated alliances in marriage, in business, and in friendship. There's no way a partnership can work with you on one side and the devil on the other. Thank you for pointing it out to me so vividly to keep me from falling into dangerous places again.

June 21

Be kind to each other, tenderhearted, forgiving one another, just as God has forgiven you because you belong to Christ (Ephesians 4:32 LB).

Father, thank you for giving me the power to forgive those who have sinned against me, and I praise you for telling me to be kind, tenderhearted, compassionate, and understanding in the same way that you are, because I belong to Christ. I love you, Jesus, for living in and through me, which gives me the power and the desire to forgive each and every person who may have ever hurt me. Father, I praise you that I don't have to keep those little hurts in my memory because of your love. Thank you that I can do this quickly, readily, and freely, because that's the way you forgave me.

June 22

Don't just pretend that you love others: really love them. Hate what is wrong. Stand on the side of the good. Love each other with brotherly affection and take delight in honoring each other. Never be lazy in your work but serve the Lord enthusiastically (Romans 12:9-11 LB).

Devil, I hate you. Father, I love you for putting in my heart such a dislike for the things of the devil, and for allowing me to hate that which is wrong. Thank you that I can stand for the good in this world. Father, I'm so appreciative of the fact that we can live in a world that says "dog eat dog" and yet we can sincerely love one another with brotherly affection because of you. I adore you, and I hate and loathe everything that is evil or ungodly, and I turn in absolute horror from wickedness. Years ago I loved wickedness, and I thank you for delivering me from that love.

June 23

If you love your neighbor as much as you love yourself you will not want to harm or cheat him, or kill him or steal from him. And you won't sin with his wife or want what is his, or do anything else the Ten Commandments say is wrong. All ten are wrapped up in this one, to love your neighbor as you love yourself (Romans 13:9 LB).

I love you, Father, because you give me the power to live the way you want me to, without wanting to harm or cheat my neighbors or steal from them. Thank you, Father, that you have wrapped up very neatly all the commandments in this one statement—love your neighbor as yourself. Thank you, Father, that I can love my neighbors because of you.

June 24

For do I now persuade men, or God? or do I seek to please men? for if I yet pleased men, I should not be the servant of Christ (Galatians 1:10).

I praise your holy name, Father, because you haven't called me to be a people pleaser, but a God pleaser. Thank you, Father, that my thoughts can be turned toward you at all times, so that I can think about pleasing you and being a servant of Jesus Christ. I thank you for allowing me to be at the beck and call of Jesus, to always do his bidding. Glory! I don't have to go along with the crowd and do things I don't want to do, because I'm afraid of what they might think about me. I'm your willing, happy, and contented servant.

June 25

To speak evil of no man. . . (Titus 3:2).

Father, let the words of my mouth be acceptable in thy sight. Let me be filled with so much of your love that my tongue will only have words that are sweet as honey. I will bridle my tongue and let no words that are harmful, hurtful, injurious, malignant, disastrous, or ruinous come out of my mouth. My lips shall speak words of love, which will bring strength, hope, and cheer to someone. I will not gossip or criticize, complain or manufacture untruths about anyone, but will keep my conversation full of your love.

June 26

Fulfil ye my joy, that ye be likeminded, having the same love, being of one accord, of one mind (Philippians 2:2).

Father, I am filling up with your love so my joy can be complete by living in harmony and being of the same mind and purpose, so that I will have the same love for all my brothers and sisters in Christ that I have for only some. I am working toward a unity with people of all denominations, so that strife, selfishness, and contentiousness will be ended. I will love those who love Jesus, even though their doctrines do not exactly agree with mine. If we are like-minded in that area, we can be in one accord and one mind. Let the little, unimportant things fall by the wayside, and let us dwell on the things that last. Thank you for giving me a love that is big enough to encompass doctrinal differences. I'm running over with love. It's splashing over on everyone I run into, and it's blessing each one it falls on, because it's your love.

June 27

Love is very patient and kind, never jealous or envious, never boastful or proud, never haughty or selfish or rude. Love does not demand its own way. It is not irritable or touchy. It does not hold grudges and will hardly even notice when others do it wrong (I Corinthians 13:4, 5 LB).

Father, thank you for the "love" chapter in the Bible. Thank you for telling us exactly what love is. Lord, we love you, because you tell us that, if we're jealous or envious, we don't have love. Thank you that when your wonderful love is flowing through us to reach others, it will never be irritable or touchy. Thank you, Father, that this is only possible because of your love. I praise you that I don't have to insist on my "rights" and on having my own way. How I bless you that I lost my grudges at the altar of salvation.

June 28

There are three things that remain—faith, hope, and love—and the greatest of these is love (I Corinthians 13:13 LB).

I praise you, Father, for the three wonderful things that remain—faith, hope, and love. Thank you that the greatest one of these is love, because without love it would be difficult to have faith and hope. With your love, because it is the greatest of all, we also have faith and hope. Faith in the knowledge that Jesus Christ is coming back, and hope that it is going to be soon. We love you, because of the joyful and confident expectation we have of eternal salvation. Thank you that you enable us to have true affection and love for you and for all people.

June 29

And hope maketh not ashamed; because the love of God is shed abroad in our hearts by the Holy Ghost which is given unto us (Romans 5:5).

Father, I thank you, because the love in my heart is not a human love that I have to generate and work up. I can spread your love all over the world, because the special love which is freely given to others has been given to us by you. It isn't anything I had to work for or beg for; it is just one of those beautiful gifts you give to your children. Thank you, Father, that the world can see your love in me. I praise you that I don't have to have unbelief or distrust, which would cause me to waver about whether or not I could really love someone, because I am empowered by my faith in you and your promises.

June 30

. . . In all these things we are more than conquerors through him that loved us (Romans 8:37).

Glory to God, I'm *more* than a conqueror. Father, how I praise you for that word *all*. Thank you for letting me know that I win *all* the battles because of your love. It was the same love that allowed Jesus Christ to die on a cross for me that makes me more than a conqueror in *all* areas of my life. Thank you that I don't have to bow to the devil in any area, because you've said, "In *all* these things we are more than conquerors through him that loved us." Thank you, Father, for another month of victory in Jesus. Thank you that I always have a surpassing victory in everything because of your great love.

July

FREEDOM FROM FEAR

As we wrote the devotions on fear, we felt a tremendous witness in our spirits that thousands of people are going to be delivered from the bondage of fear and totally and completely liberated by confessing what God's Word says about fear.

The Bible says that in the end times men's hearts will be failing them *for fear* (Luke 21:26-28), but, praise God, Revelation 21:7 also says, *He that overcometh shall inherit all things*, and we know that we have overcome the devil by the blood of the Lamb and by the word of our testimony.

Let's wake up every morning, and before we ever open our eyes, confess "*I believe, I believe, I believe!*" Then go on to confess that you believe you have been completely delivered from fear. Confess that you have been set free.

Remember, Jesus says in Mark 11:23 that you can have whatsoever you say, so let's say right now, "*I believe in total deliverance from fear!*"

Faith and fear are exact opposites. We cannot have them both at the same time, so if we're trusting God and not listening to the devil, we will have faith instead of fear. Isn't it foolish to have fear, when all we have to do when the devil sends his fiery dart of fear is to trust God. Can you imagine looking up and saying, "God, I don't trust you!" We alone can make the choice of accepting fear or accepting faith.

July 1

Be strong and courageous and get to work. Don't be frightened by the size of the task, for the Lord my God is with you; he will not forsake you. He will see to it that everything is finished correctly (I Chronicles 28:20 LB).

Today I'm strong and courageous and afraid of nothing. Thank you, Father, that you care for every little detail of my life. I am not frightened by the size of any task, because you are always with me. And how I praise you, Father, that you always see to it that every job I do is completed correctly. Thank you that I don't have to live the Christian life in my own strength, but that I can rest in you and be strengthened and assured that the work I do turns out right, because you are backing me up *all the way.*

July 2

The wicked flee when no man pursueth: but the righteous are bold as a lion (Proverbs 28:1).

Today I am bold, bold, *bold.* Father, how I praise you for giving me the boldness of a lion. Thank you that, because my righteousness comes from you, I act and make decisions with the courage that comes from knowing you are with me in all I do. Thank you, Father, that I stand up and boldly face all that comes before me in life in a way that the wicked can't imitate because of their fear that the wicked things they've done will catch up with them and destroy them. I praise you that I don't have to always be looking over my shoulder in fear as the wicked do. I get so excited, Father, when I realize I'm always on the winning side. I can charge right into any situation of the devil's making, and the wicked will flee before me, because you've made me *bold as a lion.*

July 3

For God hath not given us the spirit of fear; but of power, and of love, and of a sound mind (II Timothy 1:7).

I have a sound mind at all times, because I have the mind of Christ. I love you, praise you, thank you, and bless you, Father, because you haven't given me the spirit of fear. I rejoice that fear is never from you but is always from the devil. Because you have given me power over the devil and all his doings, I can boldly dismiss any thoughts or feelings of fear that come before me. Thank you, Father, that you've given me a sound mind and the power to face any situation and be victorious in it. I praise you, Father, for giving me the full power of your love to overcome any of the devil's confusion and darkness, because in the light of your love the shadows of fear have to run from me.

July 4

The thief cometh not, but for to steal, and to kill, and to destroy: I am come that they might have life, and that they might have it more abundantly (John 10:10).

Father, I praise you for the day you granted freedom to our nation. But more than that, I thank you for the freedom and abundance of life you have granted me through your Son, Jesus Christ, who came to defeat the devil and all the devil's evil, destructive ways. Thank you, Father, that Jesus came to free us from the bondage of the devil's fear, so that the devil can never again steal the blessings of life from your children, like the thief he really is. Thank you that Jesus is the way, the truth, and the life and that through him I have the abundant life you want all your children to have.

July 5

Behold, I give unto you power to tread on serpents and scorpions, and over all the power of the enemy: and nothing shall by any means hurt you (Luke 10:19).

Thank you, Father, that you have given me the power to tread on all the works of the devil without the slightest possibility that any harm can come to me. I rejoice that you've turned the tables on the devil, because now I have power over *all the power of the enemy,* and he has to run from me. I praise you for making me immune to the enemy's poisonous stings and fangs, because I am triumphant in times of trouble and at peace in the midst of strife. Thank you, Father, for making me a spiritual warrior, so I can stomp on the works of the enemy wherever I find them.

July 6

Roll your works upon the Lord—commit and trust them wholly to Him; [He will cause your thoughts to become agreeable to His will, and] so shall your plans be established and succeed (Proverbs 16:3 Amp.).

Father, I feel like I'm in a big bowling alley, and I've just rolled all my cares, worries, and defeats up into one big ball, and I'm rolling them all down the alley right into your arms. I'm committing them to you and trusting them wholly to you, and I'm not worrying about them any more. I thank you that my thoughts are all becoming agreeable to your will, and that nothing that comes to my mind will be unpleasing to you, because I'm turning my back on all the lusts of the flesh and rolling all of my works upon you. I'm excited, because I now have total and complete assurance that everything I do is going to be established and succeed. How I praise you that you make no plans for failure in your Word!

July 7

The Lord is my shepherd; I shall not want. He maketh me to lie down in green pastures: he leadeth me beside the still waters (Psalm 23: 1, 2).

I love and praise you, Father, because in the abiding love and care you pour upon me, I fear no evil. With you as my Shepherd, I'm surrounded by your protective power at all times. I rejoice that I can relax and enjoy your green pastures and still waters, because wherever you lead me, I have complete trust that all my needs are met. I thank you, Father, for seeing to it that I lack nothing. I praise you because I can look to you for everything I need in my life without the slightest worry or fear, for you provide for me in abundance. I bless you, Father.

July 8

Be strong and of a good courage, fear not, nor be afraid of them: for the Lord thy God, he it is that doth go with thee; he will not fail thee, nor forsake thee (Deuteronomy 31:6).

Father, I'm strong. I'm courageous. I praise you that I'm not afraid, because you are with me in all your power and glory and righteousness, and because nothing can withstand your might. I give thanks that you are the Lord my God, who never fails me or leaves me no matter what kind of difficulty or showdown I have to face. You are the strength of my arm and the courage in my heart, so I fear nothing that man can do. Glory, Father, I'm blessed with victory.

July 9

The Lord is my light and my salvation; whom shall I fear? the Lord is the strength of my life; of whom shall I be afraid? When the wicked, even mine enemies and my foes, came upon me to eat up my flesh, they stumbled and fell. Though an host should encamp against me, my heart shall not fear: though war should rise against me, in this will I be confident (Psalm 27:1-3).

I have no fear of anybody or anything. Thank you, Father, for shining your light on the path of righteousness, so I can see to walk in your ways. Thank you for saving me from sin and darkness in this life and from eternal damnation in the next, because you love me so much. You are my strength and my shield, Father, so I fear neither the wickedness of my enemies nor the tricks of the devil. You will cause them to stumble and fall without laying a finger on me. I praise you, Father, that no matter how many are in the enemy's host, I will be confident of the outcome, for your strength and power are before me, and I am triumphant. Hallelujah! You even assign your angels to minister for me.

July 10

For in the time of trouble he shall hide me in his pavilion: in the secret of his tabernacle shall he hide me; he shall set me up upon a rock (Psalm 27:5).

I rejoice, Father, that you protect and hide me from any kind of trouble that comes my way. Thank you that you always hide me in your pavilion or in the secret of your tabernacle where the wicked dare not follow. How I bless and praise you, Father, that no matter what deceitful, lying schemes the devil comes up with to disrupt my life, you'll take me out of harm's way and set me upon a rock where he can't touch me. I love you, Father.

July 11

And now shall mine head be lifted up above mine enemies round about me: therefore will I offer in his tabernacle sacrifices of joy; I will sing, yea, I will sing praises unto the Lord (Psalm 27:6).

Father, I praise you because I don't have to look up at my enemies, for you lift my head above them so that I'm looking down on them. You are the God of deliverance and the God of my salvation, Father, and I offer sacrifices of joy to you in celebration of the wonderful way you take care of me. I'm singing praises to you, because you lift me above the trials and tribulations of the world, and because I love you with all my heart. Glory!

July 12

There is therefore now no condemnation to them which are in Christ Jesus, who walk not after the flesh, but after the Spirit. For the law of the Spirit of life in Christ Jesus hath made me free from the law of sin and death (Romans 8:1, 2).

How I praise you, Father, that I fear no condemnation in my life, because there isn't any there. I rejoice because I am in Jesus Christ and I walk after the Spirit. Thank you for the promises in your Word. Your Word says that all my sins are forgiven and that you don't even remember them, so I don't have any fear of the past. I praise you, Father, that by the law of the Spirit of life in Jesus, I'm free from the law of sin and death, so that everything before me, everything in my future, is absolutely wonderful and blessed. Hallelujah!

July 13

Have not I commanded thee? Be strong and of a good courage; be not afraid, neither be thou dismayed: for the Lord thy God is with thee whithersoever thou goest (Joshua 1:9).

How I thank you, Father, that the power and truth of your commandment make me strong and fill me with courage. Fear and dismay have no part in my life, because my strength is in you and I trust you in all things. When the devil comes against me, I am brave and jubilant, for I know you are with me every moment day and night and I know I have victory over all the power of darkness. Thank you, Father, that you are with me wherever I go.

July 14

Behold, God is my salvation; I will trust, and not be afraid: for the Lord Jehovah is my strength and my song; he also is become my salvation. Therefore with joy shall ye draw water out of the wells of salvation (Isaiah 12:2, 3).

Father, I rejoice that you are my salvation. Because of this, I place my whole trust in you, and I am never afraid or anxious in anything. I rejoice in you, because you are my strength and my song. With so much confidence and happiness bubbling through me, I sing your praises everywhere I go. Father, I thank you for the wells of your salvation, because the living water I draw from them renews, blesses, and refreshes my life and gives me such joy that I feel like telling everyone I meet what a glorious God you are.

July 15

Forasmuch then as the children are partakers of flesh and blood, he also himself likewise took part of the same; that through death he might destroy him that had the power of death, that is, the devil; And deliver them who through fear of death were all their lifetime subject to bondage (Hebrews 2:14, 15).

Thank you, Father, that Jesus took death upon himself so he could destroy the one who had the power of death—the devil. Thank you that I'm free of the fear of death and free of the desperate hunger for power, money, and the things of this world that come from fearing death. I praise you, Father, that Jesus delivered me from sin, the devil, and bondage to fear by shedding his blood for me upon the cross. I thank you for that glorious promise of eternal life in your kingdom. Because death couldn't hold Jesus in the grave, it won't hold me either, and I'm rejoicing because my eternal home is in heaven with you. Thank you, Father, for the priceless blessing of eternal life.

July 16

There is no fear in love; but perfect love casteth out fear: because fear hath torment. He that feareth is not made perfect in love (I John 4:18).

I praise and thank you, glorious Father, that your perfect love flows through me in such great measure that it has cast out fear of any and all kinds. I thank you, Father, for removing the torment of fear from my life, for torment comes from the devil, and the devil has to run from the power of your perfect love. I'm blessed beyond my wildest dreams, Father, because I'm being perfected in your wonderful love.

July 17

God is our refuge and strength, a very present help in trouble. Therefore will not we fear, though the earth be removed, and though the mountains be carried into the midst of the sea; Though the waters thereof roar and be troubled, though the mountains shake with the swelling thereof. Selah (Psalm 46:1-3).

Father, I thank and praise you, because you are my refuge and strength, you are my help at the moment trouble comes. I thank you that I don't need to fear even if the world blows up and the mountains crumble into the sea, for you are the God of my salvation, and you will take care of me no matter what happens. Father, I praise you because you are the Creator, the God of everything; therefore, I don't fear anything in the entire universe. Whether the world falls apart or a great earthquake rocks the mountains, I'll be saved and protected by your loving power. Hallelujah!

July 18

I am trusting God—oh, praise his promises! I am not afraid of anything mere man can do to me! Yes, praise his promises. I will surely do what I have promised, Lord, and thank you for your help. For you have saved me from death and my feet from slipping, so that I can walk before the Lord in the land of the living (Psalm 56:10-13 LB).

Glory, Father, I trust you so much that there's no room in my life for fear. I praise your promises, for you always keep them, and I thank you for all the help you've given me. I thank you for saving me from death and for keeping my feet from slipping, so I can walk in your ways. Father, I rejoice in your light!

July 19

He that dwelleth in the secret place of the most High shall abide under the shadow of the Almighty. I will say of the Lord, He is my refuge and my fortress: my God; in him will I trust (Psalm 91:1, 2).

I thank you, Father, because I abide in the safety and comfort of your shadow where no evil can touch me. You are my refuge and my fortress, Father, and I thank you and praise you that you are a God who keeps all his promises to his children, so that my trust is always fulfilled in you. Because I dwell in the secret place of the most High, the devil can't make fear fall upon me. Instead, I am lifted up and blessed over and over by the love and power with which you surround me.

July 20

There shall not evil befall thee, neither shall any plague come nigh thy dwelling. For he shall give his angels charge over thee, to keep thee in all thy ways (Psalm 91:10, 11).

Father, thank you that no evil can befall me and no plague or sickness can come near my house, because *you said so*. Thank you that I don't have to worry about these things any more, for you've sent your angels and charged them to take care of me in every way. I praise you, Father, for loving me so much that your angels stick by me night and day to guard and protect me, my house, and my family from everything the devil might try to do to us. Thank you, Father, that your Word frees me from fear of sickness, calamity, and disease. Hallelujah!

July 21

Then he answered and spake unto me, saying, This is the word of the Lord unto Zerubbabel, saying, Not by might, nor by power, but by my spirit, saith the Lord of hosts (Zechariah 4:6). (See also in the Amplified Bible.)

Praise you, Father, that an angel of the Lord spoke to Zerubbabel and told him that the addition of the bowl to the candlestick caused it to yield a neverending supply of oil from the olive trees. Father, I bless you that oil is the symbol of your Holy Spirit, so its supply continues eternally. Thank you that I don't have to fear, because you've promised that I don't have to win battles in my own strength nor my own power, but that you will win them for me by your Spirit. Glory! Here I am, winning again!

July 22

God blesses those who obey him; happy the man who puts his trust in the Lord (Proverbs 16:20 LB).

I love to receive your blessings, Father, because I know that everything that comes from you is good. Because you are a wonderful and loving God, always faithful to your children, I trust you with all my heart. I obey you without hesitation, because everything you tell me to do comes from your righteousness, and I rejoice in your righteousness. I have no fear, nervousness, worry, or care about the future or about problems, because your blessings are upon me. I'm happy and I'm singing your praises, because I put my trust, my faith, my confidence, and my hope in you. I'm full of anticipation for the good things in life, and fear went out the window when faith and trust came in. Glory!

July 23

The Lord by wisdom hath founded the earth; by understanding hath he established the heavens. By his knowledge the depths are broken up, and the clouds drop down the dew. My son, let not them depart from thine eyes: keep sound wisdom and discretion: So shall they be life unto thy soul, and grace to thy neck. Then shalt thou walk in thy way safely, and thy foot shall not stumble. When thou liest down, thou shalt not be afraid: yea, thou shalt lie down, and thy sleep shall be sweet. Be not afraid of sudden fear, neither of the desolation of the wicked, when it cometh. For the Lord shall be thy confidence, and shall keep thy foot from being taken (Proverbs 3:19-26).

Father, I praise and thank you that your wisdom, which founded the earth, is the same wisdom that guides my life and guards me from fear of falling or of stumbling. You are my confidence, Father, and by your wisdom and knowledge there is life in my soul and grace to my neck. Father, I am awed by the magnificent miracle of your creation, and my sleep is sweet, because your children are protected day and night by your mighty power. Hallelujah!

July 24

The fear of man bringeth a snare: but whoso putteth his trust in the Lord shall be safe (Proverbs 29:25).

I thank you, Father, for taking all fear from me, because fear is just an invitation for the devil to take advantage with one of his deceitful snares. I love and praise you, Father, for being the kind of God that I can trust with all my heart, for you are always faithful to keep your children safe and filled with blessings. You are wonderful to me!

July 25

But Moses told the people, "Don't be afraid. Just stand where you are and watch, and you will see the wonderful way the Lord will rescue you today. The Egyptians you are looking at—you will never see them again. The Lord will fight for you, and you won't need to lift a finger." Then the Lord said to Moses, "Quit praying and get the people moving! Forward, march!" (Exodus 14:13-15 LB).

Father, thank you for the simplicity, directness, and power of the ways you deliver us from seemingly hopeless situations. No situation is hopeless before your mighty power. I praise you, Father, for delivering me from fear, because you are a God of wonderful miracles and faithfulness to your people. Glory!

July 26

Fear not, for I am with you. Do not be dismayed. I am your God. I will strengthen you; I will help you; I will uphold you with my victorious right hand. See, all your angry enemies lie confused and shattered. Anyone opposing you will die. You will look for them in vain—they will all be gone. I am holding you by your right hand—I, the Lord, your God—and I say to you, Don't be afraid; I am here to help you. Despised though you are, fear not, O Israel; for I will help you. I am the Lord, your Redeemer; I am the Holy One of Israel (Isaiah 41:10-14 LB).

I am thankful, Father, that you bring your people to victory no matter what the situation is. Your right hand is more powerful than all the armies of the world with all their weapons, and no one can stand against me, because you are *for me*. Thank you, Father, that I am victorious in *all situations*.

July 27

But now the Lord who created you, O Israel, says, Don't be afraid, for I have ransomed you; I have called you by name; you are mine. When you go through deep waters and great trouble, I will be with you. When you go through rivers of difficulty, you will not drown. When you walk through the fire of oppression, you will not be burned up—the flames will not consume you. For I am the Lord your God, your Savior, the Holy One of Israel. I gave Egypt and Ethiopia and Seba (to Cyrus) in exchange for your freedom, as your ransom. Others died that you might live; I traded their lives for yours because you are precious to me and honored, and I love you. Don't be afraid, for I am with you. I will gather you from east and west, from north and south. I will bring my sons and daughters back to Israel from the farthest corners of the earth. All who claim me as their God will come, for I have made them for my glory; I created them. Bring them back to me—blind as they are and deaf when I call (although they see and hear!) (Isaiah 43:1-8 LB).

How I praise you, Father, for redeeming me, for calling me by name, for rescuing me from trouble and difficulty and oppression, for saving me. Glorious Father, I rejoice that you openly declare in your Word that I am yours. Wherever I was—east, west, north, or south—you called me to yourself, because you love me, although my eyes were blind and my ears were deaf to your call. Thank you, Father, that I am precious to you and honored, for you are my God, and it is you who deserve all the glory. Because you are with me, I don't fear deep water, fire, or all the power of the devil, for you will rescue me from all of them. Father, I praise you and thank you for who you are.

July 28

Don't be afraid of those who can kill only your bodies—but can't touch your souls! Fear only God who can destroy both soul and body in hell. Not one sparrow (What do they cost? Two for a penny?) can fall to the ground without your Father knowing it. And the very hairs of your head are all numbered. So don't worry! You are more valuable to him than many sparrows (Matthew 10:28-31 LB).

How exciting, Father, to know that you love me so much you have even numbered the hairs on my head. Not only do you know how many I have, you know how many I have lost. I don't fear any person on this earth. You notice the fall of the least sparrow to the ground, so you always know when I need your help and you are instantly right there with me. I praise you, Father, for getting rid of all my worries, because you love me so much. I'm certainly glad I'm worth more to you than a sparrow!

July 29

The eternal God is thy refuge, and underneath are the everlasting arms: and he shall thrust out the enemy from before thee; and shall say, Destroy them (Deuteronomy 33:27).

Father, I give praise to you for being the eternal God, who has complete power over all things past, present, and future. I thank you for forgiving all my sins of the past, for loving me right now, and for giving me a wonderful future to look forward to. I praise you for holding me with love in your everlasting arms. Because you are my refuge, nothing can harm me regardless of the situation. Thank you for always going before me in your glory and power, so that the wicked are thrust out of my path. Father, I love your everlasting arms!

July 30

You shall also decide and decree a thing and it shall be established for you, and the light [of God's favor] shall shine upon your ways (Job 22:28 Amp.).

Bless you, Father, that I don't have to worrry about whether or not I'm going to be a failure or a success, because your blueprint for my life makes it so simple. I'm throwing fear right out the window, because you've said that when I decide and decree a thing it shall be established. How I praise you that I'm walking in the light of your favor and it's shining upon my ways. Glory, Father, what a privilege to be able to follow your Word so easily and know that you make us winners all the time. I love you for this!

July 31

Do not fret or have any anxiety about anything, but in every circumstance and in everything by prayer and petition [definite requests] with thanksgiving continue to make your wants known to God. And God's peace [be yours, that tranquil state of a soul assured of its salvation through Christ, and so fearing nothing from God and content with its earthly lot of whatever sort that is, that peace] which transcends all understanding, shall garrison and mount guard over your hearts and minds in Christ Jesus (Philippians 4:6, 7 Amp.).

How I thank and praise you, Father, because I don't worry, fret, fear, or stew about anything, for your love for me is so great that I am filled with and surrounded by your mighty power at all times. Because of your promises and your Word, I have peace in all circumstances, the peace that surpasses all understanding, the peace that guards my heart and mind in Christ Jesus. I praise you for the wonderful blessing of that peace. Hallelujah!

August

JOY

August is the time when some people begin to drag because of the long, hot summer days, but how we praise God for his Word, *But they that wait upon the Lord shall renew their strength; they shall mount up with wings as eagles; they shall run, and not be weary; and they shall walk, and not faint* (Isaiah 40:31).

Let's mount up with wings as eagles and soar higher this month than we ever have. Let's believe for the joy of the Lord during this entire month, because joy in our hearts can keep us from experiencing the doldrums that some people do. If you need joy in your life, keep asking, speaking, and believing, and it will be yours!

August 1

But they that wait upon the Lord shall renew their strength; they shall mount up with wings as eagles; they shall run, and not be weary; and they shall walk, and not faint (Isaiah 40:31).

Let's make a special prayer, agreeing with God about receiving his joy, because we're mounting up with wings as eagles. Father, today I feel like flying. I rejoice and thank you for the supernatural power and energy you give me. How I love you for telling me that when I serve and wait upon you I can mount up like an eagle and draw close to you as the eagles draw close to the sun. Thank you that when I run I'm not weary and that when I walk I don't faint. Even when I'm tired, you give me that extra energy, strength, and joy that I need. When my enthusiasm begins to lag and my zeal begins to sag, you're right there with those heavenly vitamins, which are full of joy. I'm running without any weariness and walking joyfully and erect!

August 2

These things have I spoken unto you, that my joy might remain in you, and that your joy might be full (John 15:11).

Father, how I praise you for your words, those words of hope, inspiration, assurance, and security for all the problems of life. Those words have I hidden in my heart, so that I might not sin against you. When I keep them safely tucked away in my heart as a constant reminder of your love and perfection, my joy remains, and my cup of joy is full and complete and overflowing. I thank you for this. My *joy* is full. It isn't half full; it isn't a quarter full; it's full *all the way up to the top*, because your Word says so. Today I'm going to smile at everyone I meet, and I'm going to put a smile in my voice, so that everyone I talk to will know that my joy is full and overflowing. Glory, Father, I really love you! My mouth is going to open even wider in the future to tell more and more people the Good News, so they too can be filled with your joy.

August 3

The joy of the Lord is your strength (Nehemiah 8:10).

Father, thank you that I don't have to look to any other source for my energy and strength, because you've promised that your joy is and will continue to be the strength of my life. I thank you that your joy is not something that wears me down and saps all my strength; it is the giver of abounding and endless strength. Thank you that, even though my muscles don't look like Samson's, they are just as strong because of your joy. I'm excited, Father, because I look only to you for the joy and strength of my life and to no other source. Thank you for giving me joy for my strength.

August 4

Herein is my Father glorified, that ye bear much fruit; so shall ye be my disciples. As the Father hath loved me, so have I loved you: continue ye in my love. If ye keep my commandments, ye shall abide in my love; even as I have kept my Father's commandments, and abide in his love. These things have I spoken unto you, that my joy might remain in you, and that your joy might be full (John 15:8-11).

Father, how I thank you for letting me know that the joy of Jesus would remain in me and that my joy would be full, full, *full*! It is complete and overflowing, not just a little trickle of joy. I'm so glad you want me to have the absolute maximum of joy in my life at all times. That's almost more than I can stand, but I'm willing to receive it, even though it's almost more than I am able to receive. Thank you that your desire is for me to have joy and not sorrow in my life. I praise you for this!

August 5

You have sorrow now, but I will see you again and then you will rejoice; and no one can rob you of that joy (John 16:22 LB).

Father, how I praise you that there is not a single person who can rob me of my joy. Thank you that, even though the devil does his best to step in and steal, kill, and destroy my joy, you have told me that there isn't anyone who can steal this joy, because it's Jesus' joy that's welling up in my heart. Thank you that you promise you will see me again, so I can *really* rejoice. I am overflowing with joy and am jubilant, because I'm going to see you soon.

August 6

And in that day ye shall ask me nothing. Verily, verily, I say unto you, Whatsoever ye shall ask the Father in my name, he will give it you. Hitherto have ye asked nothing in my name: ask, and ye shall receive, that your joy may be full (John 16:23, 24).

Father, how I thank you, because Jesus said I could ask you for anything in his name and you would give it to me. How I praise you that Jesus encouraged me to ask and to keep on asking, so that my joy might be full and running over. How I thank you that you are not a God of little, but a God of much, and you never want my cup of joy to have just a tiny, little bit in it. You want it to be full at all times. Thank you for being such a generous God where joy is concerned. Thank you that when my cup of joy begins to get a little empty, all I have to do is ask, and you're ready to fill it up again. Father, sometimes my cup isn't big enough to hold all the joy you give, and I thank you that you increase my capacity not only to hold more and more joy, but to enjoy the joy you give me.

August 7

Therefore the redeemed of the Lord shall return, and come with singing unto Zion; and everlasting joy shall be upon their head: they shall obtain gladness and joy; and sorrow and mourning shall flee away (Isaiah 51:11).

Father, how I thank you that I'm redeemed by the blood of the Lamb. Thank you that, because of this, everlasting joy is upon my head. I thank you that it is an *everlasting* joy, one that's going to last from now until the day Jesus comes back or until you take me home. Thank you that all sorrow and mourning shall flee away. Thank you that in the midst of all my problems, there can be tremendous joy. How I love you for giving me covenant promises.

August 8

O come, let us sing unto the Lord: let us make a joyful noise to the rock of our salvation. Let us come before his presence with thanksgiving, and make a joyful noise unto him with psalms (Psalm 95:1, 2).

Father, how I sing to you, how I thank you that you give me the privilege of making joyful noises to the rock of my salvation. Thank you that, even though I don't sound like an opera singer, or even a good country singer, you still accept the joyful noises I make to you. Thank you that I can make a joyful noise to you with psalms. I praise you because when joy is bubbling up within me in praise to you, it spills over on me, and the joy in me comes out for the world to see. I worship you, because I can come into your presence with thanksgiving, and you don't care how many times a day I do it. Thank you for just being God. No wonder I sing!

August 9

You love him even though you have never seen him; though not seeing him, you trust him; and even now you are happy with the inexpressible joy that comes from heaven itself. And your further reward for trusting him will be the salvation of your souls (I Peter 1:8 LB).

Father, thank you for letting me love Jesus even though I have never seen him. My trust in him is complete because of who he is and because of the faith that you have put in my heart to believe in him. Thank you for the joy that is so great that it cannot be expressed in words. And then to top it all off, thank you for the joy of knowing that my further reward for trusting Jesus will be the very salvation of my own soul. Lord, sometimes I think you're almost too good to us to give us so much glorious, triumphant, heavenly joy!

August 10

Just think! Though I did nothing to deserve it, and though I am the most useless Christian there is, yet I was the one chosen for this special joy of telling the Gentiles the Glad News of the endless treasures available to them in Christ (Ephesians 3:8 LB).

Father, how I praise your name that all of your joy is unmerited favor. I never did a thing to deserve it, but you chose me to share the Gospel. Thank you that just telling someone else about Jesus brings more joy into my heart than almost anything else I can think of. How I appreciate that you trust me to share the unending, boundless, fathomless, incalculable, and exhaustless riches of Christ—wealth that no human being can search out, just because I belong to you. Thank you for jubilant joy!

August 11

For the kingdom of God is not meat and drink; but righteousness, and peace, and joy in the Holy Ghost (Romans 14:17).

Father, how I bless you that your kingdom is not just eating and drinking and making merry, but it is composed of right standing with you, which brings peace into my heart that surpasses human understanding and that stays right there regardless of circumstances. Thank you, Father, that you top it all off with something better than whipped cream, because you say it's joy in the Holy Ghost. Thank you for that Holy Ghost joy. Thank you for that bubbling down inside of me that brings up joy, joy, joy. Thank you for Kingdom living!

August 12

Thou wilt show me the path of life: in thy presence is fulness of joy; at thy right hand there are pleasures for evermore (Psalm 16:11).

Father, how I praise you that you have let me personally experience the joys of this life and the exquisite pleasures of your own eternal presence. Thank you that, because you live inside me, there is a constant fullness of joy. Thank you that through your life in mine, I am able to see the pathway of life; you are a light unto my pathway and a lamp unto my feet. Thank you that I am not walking in darkness and can have joy in my heart, because I am walking in the light. How I praise you that your presence within me is a continual, growing joy that gets sweeter and sweeter with each passing day. Thank you that, because of your presence, I can walk worthy of you. I praise you that my path is the path of life and not the pathway that leads to death. Thank you that you keep my foot from slipping, because you are personally showing me the pathway of life.

August 13

Let them shout for joy, and be glad, that favour my righteous cause: yea, let them say continually, Let the Lord be magnified, which hath pleasure in the prosperity of his servant (Psalm 35:27).

Father, I'm shouting, shouting, shouting for joy. And I'm glad, glad, *glad*. I'm saying, *Let the Lord be magnified, which hath pleasure in the prosperity of his servant*. Father, how could I ever be downhearted and blue when you take personal pleasure in my prosperity? Father, my joy is boundless, because you are interested in every little nook and cranny of my entire life. Thank you for the joy you give me, because when you look in my wallet, you delight in the prosperity you have given me. Father, my tongue shall speak of your righteousness, and I shall praise you with everlasting joy all the day long.

August 14

Come, everyone, and clap for joy! Shout triumphant praises to the Lord! For the Lord, the God above all gods, is awesome beyond words; he is the great King of all the earth. He subdues the nations before us, and will personally select his choicest blessings for his Jewish people—the very best for those he loves (Psalm 47:1-4 LB).

Father, my hands are clapping with joy. I am shouting triumphant praises to you, because you are the God above all gods, and you are too wonderful for words. You are all in all. How I leap with joy, because you select the choicest of all your blessings for the children you love. Thank you, Father, that you love me. I can hardly contain my joy because of those select blessings that you have personally picked out for me. I cannot stop clapping because of you!

August 15

Let the heavens be glad, the earth rejoice; let the vastness of the roaring seas demonstrate his glory. Praise him for the growing fields, for they display his greatness. Let the trees of the forest rustle with praise. For the Lord is coming to judge the earth; he will judge the nations fairly and with truth! (Psalm 96: 11-13 LB).

Father, can you hear my heart bubbling with joy? It wells up within me so much that I can almost hear my own heart beat. I'm rejoicing and full of joy; I can even hear the seas roaring their approval and joy. My heart can hardly be contained within this human body, because *everything* in the world is singing your praises.

August 16

Light is sown for the godly and joy for the good (Psalm 97:11 LB).

Thank you for your blessings, Father, because you have taught us the laws of sowing and reaping. Thank you for telling us that what is sown is what will be reaped. Thank you that you have sown light for the godly and that it constantly surrounds me to get the darkness out of my life. Thank you, Father, that you are constantly sowing joy, joy, joy for those who are upright in heart; that joy is irrepressible and comes from your favor and protection. Thank you that your light is sown for the uncompromisingly righteous person and strewn along my pathway to light up my life. My joy cannot be contained in any container, because it is so great and unlimited; it is literally bursting out of me. Your joy is my joy, because you give it to me in such generous portions that it is more than a human can bear. But since it is divine joy, I can keep receiving and receiving and receiving it.

August 17

Always be full of joy in the Lord; I say it again, rejoice! Let everyone see that you are unselfish and considerate in all you do. Remember that the Lord is coming soon. Don't worry about anything; instead, pray about everything; tell God your needs and don't forget to thank him for his answers (Philippians 4:4-6 LB).

Father, I'm obeying your Word, and I am always full of the joy of the Lord. I am rejoicing in all circumstances and situations. I am not worrying about anything, but instead I am taking all things to you in prayer and telling you every single thing that I need. I'm thanking you in advance for the answers you have already given me and for the answers you will be giving me in the future. My joy is full to overflowing, because I have placed my trust and confidence in you.

August 18

Rejoice evermore. Pray without ceasing. In every thing give thanks: for this is the will of God in Christ Jesus concerning you (I Thessalonians 5:16-18).

Father, my joy will last forever, because I will never cease rejoicing. My prayers will last forever, because I will pray without ceasing. My thanks will last forever, because I will give thanks in everything. This is your will for me. Thank you, Father, that your will gives me more joy than my own will ever could. Thank you that you know at all times what is best for me, so that I can honestly rejoice forevermore. Thank you that I can think of you at all times, asking your advice, listening to you, and thanking you all at the same time. Father, it is wonderful how my joy surfaces all the time, because you make the directions for my life so utterly and completely simple that anyone can understand them, including me!

August 19

This is My resting place forever; here I will dwell, for I have desired it. I will abundantly bless her provision; I will satisfy her poor with bread. I will also clothe her priests with salvation, and her saints shall shout aloud for joy (Psalm 132:14-16 NKJV).

Father, I'm shouting today with joy. And I'm shouting loud and clear, so that the world can hear me. My joy overflows and runs all over those with whom I come in contact today. Because your promises are so overflowing and so abundant, there is no way I could ever contain my joy in this earthly container without verbally expressing it and letting the whole world know that the saints shall shout aloud for joy. I praise you, Father, that you give me divine permission to shout aloud, regardless of what the world might say or think about my being noisy. I'm doing it because of your abundant provisions!

August 20

I will greatly rejoice in the Lord, my soul shall be joyful in my God; for He has clothed me with the garments of salvation, He has covered me with the robe of righteousness, as a bridegroom decks himself with ornaments, and as a bride adorns herself with her jewels (Isaiah 61:10 NKJV).

I am joyful, Father, as I look at the garments of salvation with which you have clothed me and at the robe of righteousness with which you have covered me from the top of my head to the soles of my feet. Father, I thank you that the robes and garments you have given me are as beautiful as any bridegroom bedecked with ornaments or as any bride adorned with jewels for her wedding day. I glory in your righteousness with which you have covered me. My soul can hardly contain the joy that bubbles up continually because of your gifts to me.

August 21

Your words were found, and I ate them, and Your word was to me the joy and rejoicing of my heart; For I am called by Your name, O Lord God of hosts (Jeremiah 15:16 NKJV).

Father, your joy delights my soul. I praise you for allowing my joy to overcome and overwhelm all things in my life. I discovered that when I eat your words there is an automatic bubbling up of everlasting joy and an eternal rejoicing in my heart. My joy is in your Word, Father, because it contains the blueprint for my life and your promises, which are mine when I do what you tell me to do. Father, you are such a bountiful Giver through your Word that joy and rejoicing are constant in my heart. Thank you that I am called by your wonderful, holy, magnificent, all-powerful name. Glory!

August 22

But let all those rejoice who put their trust in You; let them ever shout for joy, because You defend them; let those also who love Your name be joyful in You. For You, O

Lord, will bless the righteous; with favor You will surround him as with a shield (Psalm 5:11, 12 NKJV).

Father, I rejoice because my trust is in you. There is no one or no single thing that I would ever trust except you, so I can shout with joy, because you defend me. My heart is bubbling over with joy, because you bless the righteous. Joy wells up within me, because you surround me with favor as with a shield. I thank you that I have favor not only with you, but I also have favor with people. Father, this causes my joy to be something that cannot be compressed, held down, or even held in, because your blessings surround me at all times. My joy continues day and night, because you encompass me with a shield of righteousness at all times. Thank you that loving you allows me to be joyful at all times. I'm shouting the word of joy to a lonesome world!

August 23

Looking unto Jesus, the author and finisher of our faith, who for the joy that was set before Him endured the cross, despising the shame, and has sat down at the right hand of the throne of God (Hebrews 12:2 NKJV).

Father, how we maintain joy at all times, because you gave us Jesus, the author and finisher of our faith. Father, joy wells up within us, because, even though Jesus endured the cross and despised the shame he had to go through, he looked beyond all that and saw the joy that was at the end of his suffering. Father, thank you that he received joy when he looked down the line and saw that his life would be reproduced in mine. That joy was great, and that is why I can always have great and mighty joy that is not dependent on circumstances or the things that I can see, hear, taste, touch, or smell. My joy is based on his completed work at Calvary.

August 24

"This is the covenant that I will make with them after those days, says the Lord: I will put My laws into their hearts, and in their minds I will write them," then He adds, "Their sins and their lawless deeds I will remember no more" (Hebrews 10:16, 17 NKJV).

Father, I am exuberant today because of the joy that has come into my heart from the covenant you have made with me. How overwhelmed I am with total joy, because you have put your laws into my very own heart and you have written them indelibly in my mind, actually going into my innermost thoughts and understanding. Father, when I think about the complete meaning of your words when you say you will *never* remember my sins or my lawless deeds again, I am overcome with joy. I have joy unspeakable when I realize that you have given me absolute remission for my sins and have completely cancelled them!

August 25

Blessed be the Lord, who daily loads us with benefits, the God of our salvation! (Psalm 68:19 NKJV).

Father, the joy in my heart is unending and is a daily experience, because every day you bear our burdens and every day you load us down with your benefits and blessings. Father, there is such joy in my heart that I am in high spirits all the time. As a result, I will praise the name of God with a song and will magnify him with thanksgiving at all times, because I cannot keep the joy to myself. Father, I thank you that your blessings are not given only one time—nor are they given just once a year or once a month—but they are a *daily occurrence.* I have joy in my heart, because you don't just give us a little sampling of benefits; you give us an overabundance of everything, including joy!

August 26

The steps of a good man are ordered by the Lord; and he delighteth in his way (Psalm 37:23).

Father, I'm stepping, stepping higher and higher in joy, because I'm walking in the steps you have ordered. My joy is in high gear, because you direct each and every step I take. My joy is complete, because I don't have to worry about the direction I'm going, since you personally order me to take each step. How can I help but be full of joy? The way you direct my steps is so sure and true, so superior to anything I could ever do to find my own way. How I rejoice with great joy, because it doesn't make any difference if I'm going east, west, north, or south; you guide my footsteps in the *right* direction. Joy overwhelms me, because you are not only interested in my entire trip through life, but you are interested in every single step I take!

August 27

God is my strength and my power: and he maketh my way perfect (II Samuel 22:33).

Father, how I wake up with joy every morning because *you* are my strength and my power. Thank you that I can have joy and that I do not have to be satisfied with the things of this world and with my own strength. Joy comes because you have given me your very own strength and power; this is the way you make my ways perfect. Father, how I praise you that I can have joy in my life even on those days when my energy seems to lag and everything seems to sag. You give me joy through the mighty energy that Jesus Christ puts in me, energizing and empowering me to do what he wants me to do. I rejoice in the fact that you are my strong fortress and that, because you guide me, you set me free. Joy comes in the morning; joy comes in the afternoon; joy comes in the evening!

August 28

Knowing this, that our old man is crucified with him, that the body of sin might be destroyed, that henceforth we should not serve sin. For he that is dead is freed from sin (Romans 6:6, 7).

Father, I traded sin for joy. What a wonderful trade I made. Sin made me miserable, and joy makes me glad. Father, I rejoice in the fact that I can go to my own spiritual funeral and see myself dead to sin. Joy abounds in my life, because in our dying to self you have totally and completely removed us from sin. I rejoice in the end of self. Father, my joy knows no bounds, because you made it possible for me never to live in the flesh again but to always walk in the Spirit, so that I would not fulfill the lusts of the flesh. Father, how I thank you for the joy, the pleasure, and the delight that fill and fulfill my life at all times!

August 29

Finally, brethren, whatsoever things are true, whatsoever things are honest, whatsoever things are just, whatsoever things are pure, whatsoever things are lovely, whatsoever things are of good report; if there be any virtue, and if there be any praise, think on these things (Philippians 4:8).

Father, you and the devil don't go together, and neither do sadness and joy. How I take pleasure and delight in being able to think on the things of your Kingdom and not on the things and the problems of this world. My joy and my constant pleasure are to follow your Word and keep my mind centered on all the things you have so plainly told me would keep me in the joy of the Lord. I praise you and rejoice that I don't have to be in a continual state of being disturbed and tormented, but I have the great privilege of thinking on the beautiful, uplifting things that are true, honest, just, pure, and lovely. Joy comes in following your simple directions!

August 30

The Spirit of the Lord is upon me, because he hath anointed me to preach the gospel to the poor; he hath sent me to heal the brokenhearted, to preach deliverance to the captives, and recovering of sight to the blind, to set at liberty them that are bruised (Luke 4:18).

Father, what a perfect job description you have given us. What a joy it is to know exactly what my job is on this earth. I think of the years when I wondered why I was born and what my purpose was on this earth. You have made it so plain and clear that I can be full of your joy at all times, because you have given me such a complete blueprint to follow. I rejoice in the fact that your anointing is here at all times, whether I feel like it or not. Thank you for giving me such an exciting, joyful job!

August 31

And they overcame him by the blood of the Lamb, and by the word of their testimony: and they loved not their lives unto the death (Revelation 12:11).

Father, there's joy in the heart of a winner. There's joy in the heart of an overcomer. There's joy in the heart of a person who is always triumphant. Thank you that you cause us to be triumphant at all times. Joy reigns supreme in my heart, because you have made me to always be in the winner's circle. You have made us to be overcomers always, always, *always* and in *all* situations. Joy wells up in my heart, because I know that the very word of my testimony puts me in the winner's circle, eligible for all the blue ribbons that are going to be given out. Joy flows like the blood of Jesus, because it is that very life-giving blood that makes this all possible. Thank you for giving me another full month of being an overcomer!

September

HEALING

Healing Is for *You!*

For verily I say unto you, That whosoever shall say unto this mountain, Be thou removed, and be thou cast into the sea; and shall not doubt in his heart, but shall believe that those things which he saith shall come to pass; ***He shall have whatsoever he saith*** (Mark 11:23).

Beloved, this is the month to speak for our healing. God's Word says that we can have whatsoever we say, and in the name of Jesus, we speak healing for you this month.

When we speak sickness, we have sickness.
When we speak poverty, we have poverty.
When we speak problems, we have problems.

But . . .

When we speak healing, we *have* healing.
When we speak prosperity, we *have* prosperity.
When we speak answers, we *have* answers.

God said it, so it is true. We are called on to speak the things that we need in our lives. If it's healing you need this month, place your hand right here, and we'll believe with you for that healing.

Father, in the name of Jesus, we accept your promise that we can have whatsoever we say. We speak healing for our friends who are reading this right now. Father, we ask your healing power to come down on them in such a way that it will cover them from the top of their head to the tips of their toes, and that even at this moment they will feel the warmth of your love and healing. We thank you, Father, and praise you, for their healing at this very moment, in the name of Jesus!

September 1

Bless the Lord, O my soul, and forget not all his benefits: Who forgiveth all thine iniquities; who healeth all thy diseases (Psalm 103:2, 3).

Father, I praise you for being the God who loves us so much that you even remind us in your Word not to forget *all* your benefits. Father, don't ever let me forget a single one of them, because I rejoice with open arms to receive all the blessings you want me to have. I thank you that all my *sins* are gone, gone, *gone*, and that you have healed *all* my diseases. I'm walking in divine health, and I praise you for it. Thank you for redeeming my life from the pit and corruption and for beautifying me with your lovingkindness and tender mercies!

September 2

He sent his word, and healed them, and delivered them from their destructions (Psalm 107:20).

Thank you, Father, for sending your Word to heal us. Thank you that there is no sickness in your Kingdom, and we don't have to be in bondage to disease and illness. I love you, Father, because the prescription to heal every disease is written in your Word. Thank you that we're delivered from all our destructions and healed of all our physical problems. Thank you for sending your Word of healing and deliverance. Thank you that not one word of all your good promises has failed—in the past, the present, or the future. I love you and worship you for this!

September 3

If thou wilt diligently hearken to the voice of the Lord thy God, and wilt do that which is right in his sight, and wilt give ear to his commandments, and keep all his statutes, I will put none of these diseases upon thee, which I have brought upon the Egyptians: for I am the Lord that healeth thee (Exodus 15:26).

I'm listening carefully, Father, and I praise you for talking long enough for me to hear your voice and for keeping your Holy Spirit constantly after me, so that I will do what is right. Thank you for ears that hear, and thank you for the promise that you won't put any of the diseases you gave the Egyptians on me. Thank you, Lord, that you bring Good News and healing. I praise you for being a disease-free God!

September 4

He was wounded for our transgressions, he was bruised for our iniquities: the chastisement of our peace was upon him; and with his stripes we are healed (Isaiah 53:5).

I thank you, Father, for your wonderful Word of prophecy through Isaiah who predicted the suffering of your Son years before it happened. Thank you for the wounds that covered our transgressions. How I love Jesus for taking the bruises for our iniquities and the chastisement of our peace. Jesus, we can never thank you enough for that, but we keep doing our best. Thank you, Jesus, that those stripes on your back were taken for my healing. I praise you, Father, that I am healed because of the miracle of miracles that took place 2,000 years ago.

September 5

That it might be fulfilled which was spoken by Esaias the prophet, saying, Himself took our infirmities, and bare our sicknesses (Matthew 8:17).

How we bless you and praise you, Father, that Jesus took every one of our infirmities and he accepted all our sicknesses upon himself. We praise you, Father, that he didn't leave some of them out, but that he just made one big, clean sweep of all the sicknesses in the entire world and bore each and every one of them for us. Thank you, Father, that because Jesus did this, we don't have to have sickness. There's just no point in both of us having it. I'm not accepting sickness in my body, because then Jesus' sacrifice would have been in vain!

September 6

My son, attend to my words; incline thine ear unto my sayings. Let them not depart from thine eyes; keep them in the midst of thine heart. For they are life unto those that find them, and health to all their flesh (Proverbs 4:20-22).

Father, I'm listening. I'm attending to your Word. I've got my ear turned to you and tuned in to you. I've got my eyes glued to your words, and I'm not going to let them get out of my sight. I'm feeding on your Word, so it becomes a vital part of me, right in the midst of my heart. I praise you for the life that you have given to me through your Word and for the health that I'm enjoying every day. I bless you, Father!

September 7

Who his own self bare our sins in his own body on the tree, that we, being dead to sins, should live unto righteousness: by whose stripes ye were healed (I Peter 2:24).

Thank you, Father, for the cross where Jesus died, where he took upon himself all our sins, so that I don't have a sin left against me. I praise you that he took each and every one of them and bore them, so that I can and do live in your righteousness. How I love you for giving us that health through those stripes he endured, so that we could say, "Healing is mine!" Father, I praise you. I will confess those words over and over again, "By his stripes I was healed. By his stripes I was healed. By his stripes I was healed." Hallelujah!

September 8

I have heard thy prayer, I have seen thy tears; behold, I will heal thee (II Kings 20:5).

Heavenly Father, thank you for looking down at me and seeing my tears. I don't understand how you could see each and every single tear I've cried, because they've been so many, but I praise you that not a single one of them escaped you. I don't fully understand all your promises, but how I praise you that you so simply told me you would heal me. I love you, Father. From the innermost recesses of my heart, I thank you that you *have heard* my prayers, as insignificant or as improperly worded as they might have been. Glory!

September 9

And the Lord will take away from thee all sickness, and will put none of the evil diseases of Egypt, which thou knowest, upon thee; but will lay them upon all them that hate thee (Deuteronomy 7:15).

Father, I'm healed before I get sick. Hallelujah! I praise you, Father, for taking away from me all illness and disease, because you love and protect those who are faithful to you. I praise you that, instead, you lay diseases on those who hate me, because those who hate your servants fall under your judgment; and your judgment is righteous. Thank you, Father, that your Word promises that you will take away from me *all sickness* not just some sicknesses. I rejoice in the wonderful health you have given me, heavenly Father!

September 10

A merry heart doeth good like a medicine: but a broken spirit drieth the bones (Proverbs 17:22).

Father, I'm laughing right now. Ha, ha, ha, ho, ho, ho, he, he, he, because you said that laughter does us good like a medicine. I thank you for the dose of heavenly medicine that cures ills. Father, I'm going to laugh all day long, because a merry heart brings healing like a medicine. Thank you for letting us know that we should have a good sense of humor. Thank you that I don't have to have a depressed mind or a broken spirit, which dries up my bones, because you have renewed me. Thank you, Father, that we can give our brothers and sisters in Christ a dose of medicine when they need it by cheering their hearts with laughter. Ha, ha, ha, ho, ho, ho, he, he, he!

September 11

Large crowds followed Jesus as he came down the hillside. Look! A leper is approaching. He kneels before him, worshiping. "Sir," the leper pleads, "if you want to, you can heal me." Jesus touches the man. "I want to," he says. "Be healed." And instantly the leprosy disappears (Matthew 8:1-3 LB).

"I want to." "I want to." "I want to." What wonderful words of life those are! How I praise you, Father, that Jesus *wants* to heal us. I love you because it is in the very heart of Jesus to *want* us to have all the good things in life. I bless you because your Word tells us that Jesus has no desire for us to be sick, because he *wants* to heal us. I praise you, Father, because you are a God who wants us in perfect and divine health.

September 12

Behold, I am the Lord, the God of all flesh: is there any thing too hard for me? (Jeremiah 32:27).

Father, I love you and praise you because you are the God of *all* flesh. I praise you that you never do things half way; you always go all the way. I love you for this, Father. I'm so glad that nothing is too hard for you. I praise you that when my own situations become so big they overwhelm me, I can give them to you and rest safe and secure in the knowledge that *nothing* is too hard for *you*. Father, I worship you, because that which I think is an unsurmountable mountain is just a stack of children's blocks that can easily be knocked over by you. Hallelujah!

September 13

If you do these things, God will shed his own glorious light upon you. He will heal you; your godliness will lead you forward, and goodness will be a shield before you, and the glory of the Lord will protect you from behind. Then, when you call, the Lord will answer. "Yes, I am here," he will quickly reply (Isaiah 58:8-9 LB).

Thank you, Father, for that glorious light you shed upon me. I thank you for your promises of healing and restoration. I thank you that your godliness leads me forward and your goodness is just like a shield for me, bringing me peace and prosperity. Thank you that you're always there when I call, and thank you that you so quickly reply, "I am here!" Glory, Father, I'm overcome with your promises. Thank you for removing every form of false and wicked speaking and for guiding me continually.

September 14

The fear of the Lord prolongeth days: but the years of the wicked shall be shortened (Proverbs 10:27).

Heavenly Father, I praise you that my life is long. Thank you that, because I love you and stand in awe of your majesty and greatness, you lengthen my days. I praise you that only the wicked will have their days shortened, because your Word says, *The wages of sin is death*. I rejoice that we have favor with you, that you bless our days with health and peace of mind, that you reward the lives of the righteous. Thank you for always blessing me with all the good things in life. I love you!

September 15

There is that speaketh like the piercings of a sword: but the tongue of the wise is health (Proverbs 12:18).

I praise you, Father, for giving me a wise tongue. I bless you because you have taught me to speak divine health. I praise you that you've taught me not to let any corrupt communication come out of my mouth and not to acknowledge the sickness of the devil, but instead I can confidently say, "I'm catching a healing!" when the devil tries to give me a cold. Father, I praise you because my own tongue brings your health into my life. I bless you for this! I thank you that a wise tongue speaks your Word, which brings healing to the body. Thank you for harnessing my tongue to bring it under control.

September 16

A wholesome tongue is a tree of life: but perverseness therein is a breach in the spirit (Proverbs 15:4).

Father, my tongue is wholesome. I praise you that you are the one who has made this possible. I thank you that my tongue is a tree of life that brings health and happiness. Father, because you control my tongue, I don't break down my spirit with contrary words. Thank you that I've given up the griping that brings discouragement, because the words you speak through my mouth are gentle and have healing power. I love you for this, Father.

September 17

And ye shall serve the Lord your God, and he shall bless thy bread, and thy water; and I will take sickness away from the midst of thee. There shall nothing cast their young, nor be barren, in thy land: the number of thy days I will fulfil (Exodus 23:25, 26).

I praise you, Father, that my bread is blessed and so is my water. I thank you that you have taken sickness away from me and my family. I thank you that women can stand on your Word and not have miscarriages. I praise you that you have promised that the wombs of your children will not be barren. Thank you for every person who has been wanting a baby, who can now claim that promise, because they are serving you. I praise you, Father, for making the barren women the joyful mothers of many children. Glory!

September 18

He taught me also, and said unto me, Let thine heart retain my words: keep my commandments, and live (Proverbs 4:4).

Father, I love you and praise you, because your words are written in my heart. I'm keeping them there by memorizing and confessing them. Because I know what your Word says, I'm keeping your commandments. Thank you, Father, that your Word has told me if I do this I will have a long and happy life. I'm holding fast to every word you have said. I'm confessing all your promises, and I'm hiding them in the deepest recesses of my heart. I'm hiding them there so I won't sin against you, Father.

September 19

He healeth the broken in heart, and bindeth up their wounds (Psalm 147:3).

Father, I thank you that, even though my heart has been broken into many parts, you put it all back together again. Thank you that you didn't leave me all alone to gather up the pieces, but you gathered them all up for me and put them together in a whole and complete heart. Thank you that I didn't have to go into a corner and lick my wounds like a dog, because your loving care binds them up for me. Thank you for curing all my pains and all my sorrows. Thank you for those divine bandages with that everlasting healing power in them that you wrap around all my wounds. Hallelujah, Father, I love you for this!

September 20

And the prayer of faith shall save the sick, and the Lord shall raise him up; and if he have committed sins, they shall be forgiven him (James 5:15).

Heavenly Father, thank you that I can pray for myself, and yet I can also have others pray for me, because you simply said the "prayer of faith" would heal the sick. Father, I praise you that when I am too sick to pray for myself, I can depend on my friends and brothers and sisters in Christ to pray the prayer of faith for me. Thank you that you raise me up from my sick bed, and that, if there's any sin in my life, you forgive me. Father, I praise you for the most wonderful life in the world—the Christian life.

September 21

I shall not die, but live, and declare the works of the Lord (Psalm 118:17).

I praise you, glorious Father, for your Word that you have given us to stand on. Thank you for such a promise as this one, which I can rely on and declare to the world. Your works are truly magnificent and wonderful. Thank you that, even though the doctors tell me I have an incurable disease and that there is nothing they can do, I can declare your Word and know that I shall not die, but live, and declare the wonderful works you have done for me. Thank you, Father, for your positive promises, which give hope to the most weak in heart. Father, I boldly declare your works. Glory!

September 22

But for you who fear my name, the Sun of Righteousness will rise with healing in his wings. And you will go free, leaping with joy like calves let out to pasture (Malachi 4:2 LB).

Father, I bless and praise you, because there's healing in the wings of the Sun of Righteousness. I praise you that there are blessings in his wings, and one of them is healing. Thank you for setting me free, so I can leap with joy like a calf let out to pasture. Father, no worldly joy compares with the joy I have because of the healing in those wings. Glory! I will continually praise you and respect and have awe for your name because of your good promises to *all* your children.

September 23

For I will restore health unto thee, and I will heal thee of thy wounds, saith the Lord (Jeremiah 30:17).

I praise you, Father, for another of your positive promises, that you will restore health to me. I praise you that you didn't say you would have to think about it; you simply said that you would restore health to me. Thank you that you heal me of all my wounds, whether they are of the body, mind, or spirit. I rejoice that I can worship you and serve you as a whole, healthy person. Father, thank you for the best promises in the whole world. Thank you for being the best promise-giver and the best promise-keeper in the entire world. I love you for this.

September 24

Be not wise in your own eyes; reverently fear and worship the Lord, and turn (entirely) away from evil. It shall be health to your nerves and sinews, and marrow and moistening to your bones (Proverbs 3:7, 8 Amp.).

Father, I thank you that I don't have to be smart in my own eyes. I worship you, I praise you, I love you, I adore you. Because of you I turn entirely and completely away from all sin and evil. Thank you that, because you taught me this, I have health to my nerves and sinews and life-giving blood in the marrow of my bones. Thank you that my bones aren't dry and brittle but are moist and pliable, so I can reach out and accept your gift of health. I love you, Father!

September 25

Blessings on all who reverence and trust the Lord—on all who obey him! Their reward shall be prosperity and happiness. Your wife shall be contented in your home. And look at all those children! There they sit around the dinner table as vigorous and healthy as young olive trees. That is God's reward to those who reverence and trust him (Psalm 128:1-4 LB).

Thank you, Father, that I have your blessings, because I reverence, trust, and obey you. How we praise you for healthy children! Because we love you, you reward us even on this earth by giving us children as strong and healthy as young olive trees. Thank you, Father, for including healthy children in your promised reward of prosperity and happiness to those who love and serve you. We rejoice in telling our children that it's you—our Father in heaven—who blesses, protects, and prospers us. Glory, Father!

September 26

And the eyes of them that see shall not be dim, and the ears of them that hear shall hearken (Isaiah 32:3).

Father, I praise you that you have given me eyes that see and ears that hear, for your Word says I have them. Because my eyes are not dim in spiritual matters, I am not fooled by the devil's temptations. Because my ears are not deaf in spiritual things, I am not deceived by the devil's wicked lies. I see and hear correctly, because you have blessed me with physical health and spiritual discernment. I praise you for this, Father. You are a wonderful God, loving, merciful, and powerful.

September 27

There shall no evil befall thee, neither shall any plague come nigh thy dwelling (Psalm 91:10).

Thank you, Father, for protecting me from all illness and disease, because your Word promises that you won't let any evil or plague overtake me. I thank you for protection from colds, flu, boils, infections, and plagues of any kind. Father, you are my physician, and you have the best hospitalization plan in the world, which is for us to stay healthy. I praise you that you can heal anything that befalls us, and I love you for keeping me healthy, so I don't have to get healed. Thank you for divine health. Thank you for divine protection from accidents, too, Father, because accidents fall under the heading of evil. Thank you for that blood barrier around me that protects me from wicked tongues as well. Thank you for protection of *all* kinds!

September 28

And when I passed by thee, and saw thee polluted in thine own blood, I said unto thee when thou was in thy blood, Live; yea, I said unto thee when thou wast in thy blood, Live (Ezekiel 16:6).

Father, thank you for protection from hemorrhaging during childbirth or any other time. I praise and thank you that when my blood flows from me during an attack from the devil, I can stand on the rock of your Word and know that you say to me, "Live!" Thank you for loving us so much that you want us to be healthy, whole, and protected throughout our bodies. I praise you, heavenly Father, that when we see a brother or sister in distress or trouble from bleeding, we can use your Word and command hemorrhaging to stop. I love you, Father.

September 29

So shall they fear the name of the Lord from the west, and his glory from the rising of the sun. When the enemy shall come in like a flood, the Spirit of the Lord shall lift up a standard against him (Isaiah 59:19).

How we thank you, Father, for your constant protection of our health and well-being. Thank you for letting us know that the enemy is going to try to attack us over and over and over. But when he does come in like a flood, and it seems as though we might be swept away by the undertow of his wickedness, your Spirit is always there to lift up a standard against him. We praise you for your protection, your constant care, and your loving-kindness from the rising of the sun to the going down of the same!

September 30

O Lord my God, I cried unto thee, and thou hast healed me (Psalm 30:2).

Father, how we praise you that when our health has sagged or even seems to be gone completely, we can cry out to you and you heal us. I love you, Father, because when we get wounded in the battle of health, no matter how deep or painful those wounds are, you have promised in your Word to heal us. I praise you, Father, because things that are impossible with men are possible with you. You are a God of love and truth and victory, and I rejoice in your miraculous healing power and glorify you for it. Thank you for another month of victorious health. I thank you and praise you, because your promises that I've confessed this month are true. Glory, Father!

October

HOLY SPIRIT

October is the month of *power*! If you've never received the power of the Christian life, which is the baptism with the Holy Spirit, you *will* after confessing the Word this month on the Holy Spirit.

To us, the Holy Spirit has always been the "double portion." We can all pray in our native language, but praying with the Spirit is that double portion we all want and need.

One of the biggest surprises came when we realized there was a difference between the "gift of tongues" and the "prayer of tongues." This really helped clear up some of the confusion. We had always put them into one category—that of "speaking in tongues"—and *never* realized any difference at all, nor did we associate this with the power of the Holy Spirit. No wonder we thought, "Do all speak in tongues?" applied to us negatively.

Praise God for his grace, because we are beginning to be more and more aware of the complete misunderstanding that exists concerning the outward sign of having been baptized with the Holy Spirit. Many people who praise God in their own private language have never received the "gift" of tongues to the assembly, and many never will.

Compare the difference between the "praise and prayer" tongue, which is for all, and the gift of tongues, which is to the assembly and is not for all. When the anointing falls upon a person with a message *from* God, it is a message from heaven to earth. This is a message from God to his people, and in order for the congregation to understand it, it must be followed by an interpretation into the language they understand. The person who has the "gift" or "job" of interpretation has another gift to be manifested in partnership with the tongues spoken out. He or she receives the interpretation from God and transmits it to the congregation in their language.

Now think back on what the "praise" tongue is. It is just the reverse of the "public" tongue. It does not need an interpretation, because it is a prayer of intercession by the Holy Spirit directly to God. He is all wisdom and all knowledge. He understands all languages, so he does not need anyone to interpret for him. The prayer is to him and him alone and is not to be shared with anyone on the earth. Remember this is "earth to heaven" conversation (see I Corinthians 14:2). The other is "heaven to earth" conversation, and there is a difference! (See I Corinthians 12:10.)

October 1

But ye shall receive power, after that the Holy Ghost is come upon you: and ye shall be witnesses unto me both in Jerusalem, and in all Judaea, and in Samaria, and unto the uttermost part of the earth (Acts 1:8).

I have power! Do you know how I know this, Father? Because your wonderful Word says so! I have ability, efficiency, and might because of your Holy Spirit. I thank you that the Holy Spirit not only fills me, but is completely diffused throughout my very own soul. How I praise you for completely immersing and submerging me in the power of your Holy Spirit. How I bless you for giving me the boldness of a lion to speak and share the Good News at all times. I'm talking to my neighbors. I'm talking to my fellow employees. I'm talking to the people I do business with. Father, I'm so bold today I'm going to share your Word with everyone I meet. Glory!

October 2

If ye then, being evil, know how to give good gifts unto your children: how much more shall your heavenly Father give the Holy Spirit to them that ask him? (Luke 11:13).

I thank you, Father, that you never give us anything evil. I love you and praise you, because everything you give to me is good. I always want to give the best to my children, and I thank you, Father, that you want to give the best to me. I'm so glad that you love me more than I could ever love a member of my family, and that you give me better gifts than I could ever hope to give my loved ones. I thank you that I am loved by you and that you have given me the gift of your precious Holy Spirit. Thank you that I don't have to speculate and wonder if it's good or evil, but that I *know, know, know* that it is good, because it is from you. Glory!

October 3

And suddenly there came a sound from heaven as of a rushing mighty wind, and it filled all the house where they were sitting. And there appeared unto them cloven tongues like as of fire, and it sat upon each of them. And they were all filled with the Holy Ghost, and began to speak with other tongues, as the Spirit gave them utterance (Acts 2:2-4).

Heavenly Father, I love you, because the rushing sound that came on the day of Pentecost came right from heaven. I thank you that it fell upon *all* who were there, and they were *all* filled with the Holy Spirit, and they all began to speak in tongues as the Spirit gave them utterance. I thank you, Father, because you haven't changed your plan and you don't restrict the Holy Spirit to just a few, but you give it unselfishly to *all* of us. Father, I praise you for loving me just as much as you loved the disciples and for giving me the same beautiful gift of the Holy Spirit!

October 4

I indeed baptize you with water unto repentance: but he that cometh after me is mightier than I, whose shoes I am not worthy to bear: he shall baptize you with the Holy Ghost, and with fire (Matthew 3:11).

I'm on fire, Father, but I don't call the fire department. I want to keep this fire burning. I praise you that your promises have come down through the ages, so that I too could receive the same baptism that the disciples did on the day of Pentecost. I thank you that the fire of the Holy Spirit burns out the chaff in my life but cannot itself be put out or burned out. I bless you and praise you, because this indwelling power enables me to live above the sin of the world with a complete dislike and distaste for the things of the world.

October 5

. . . Walk in the Spirit, and ye shall not fulfil the lust of the flesh (Galatians 5:16).

I'm walking and leaping and praising God in the Spirit! Thank you, Father, for making your Word so simple for me to understand. I'm responsive to and controlled and guided by your Holy Spirit, and I'm walking, talking, and living in the Holy Spirit at all times. You alone empower me to do this, because you enable me to look at the lust of the flesh without gratifying those desires that are of my human nature and not of you. I don't have to listen to the devil when he talks to me, because I'm walking in the Spirit in power and glory and overcoming the devil all the way. How I praise and love you!

October 6

Likewise the Spirit also helpeth our infirmities: for we know not what we should pray for as we ought: but the Spirit itself maketh intercession for us with groanings which cannot be uttered. And he that searcheth the hearts knoweth what is the mind of the Spirit, because he maketh intercession for the saints according to the will of God (Romans 8:26, 27).

Glory, Father, I'm praying according to your perfect will. How do I know I am? Because your Word says so. How I bless you that you have given me such a beautiful prayer language with which to pray. Sometimes the problems of the world are so great upon my shoulders, I don't know which way to turn, and I don't know what words to say, so I just pray in the Spirit, and he intercedes for me. How I bless you that in the natural I might pray outside of your will, but in the Spirit I always pray in perfect harmony with your perfect will. How I praise you, Father, that the Holy Spirit rushes to my aid *at all times!*

October 7

Wherefore be ye not unwise, but understanding what the will of the Lord is. And be not drunk with wine, wherein is excess; but be filled with the Spirit (Ephesians 5:17, 18).

Father, I'm filled up all the way to the top and running over with your Spirit. I praise you for letting me be wise in your ways, so I will know what your will is. Thank you for that personal advice about not being drunk with wine. I think of the times before I was saved when I was drunk on the wine of the world, but I praise you because my spirit can soar higher and be stimulated more with the new wine of the Spirit than it ever did on artificial means. Father, I love you for giving me power to know your will.

October 8

But the Comforter, which is the Holy Ghost, whom the Father will send in my name, he shall teach you all things, and bring all things to your remembrance, whatsoever I have said unto you (John 14:26).

Father, how I praise you that the Holy Spirit is my teacher. Thank you that the Holy Spirit is the Comforter, the Counselor, the Helper, the Intercessor, the Advocate, the Strengthener, and the Standby in all situations. I thank you that the Holy Spirit was sent to magnify Jesus. I thank you for not limiting the Holy Spirit to teaching me certain truths, but for sending him to teach me all things and to bring *all* of what your Word says to my remembrance. Thank you, Father, that I can trust what the Holy Spirit brings to my mind, because it is *all* good and *all* from you. Thank you for being so good to me.

October 9

Whosoever drinketh of the water that I shall give him shall never thirst; but the water that I shall give him shall be in him a well of water springing up into everlasting life (John 4:14).

I'm drinking at the springs of living water, and I'm happy. I praise you, Father, for the living water. I love you for giving the living water to me because I never get parched or thirsty as long as I drink from that water. I thank you and praise you that it is a well within my very own soul that springs up into everlasting life. Father, I praise you that you took me out of all the dry years I spent with the devil, and that you put me where I shall never thirst again. Thank you for that well of water that is constantly welling up, flowing, and bubbling continually within me unto eternal life.

October 10

And I will pray the Father, and he shall give you another Comforter, that he may abide with you for ever (John 14:16).

Father, I love you, love you, love you for giving me another Comforter; but even more than this, Father, I praise you because you have promised that he will abide with me forever and forever and forever. I praise you and thank you that the Holy Spirit is abiding in me right now, comforting me and accompanying me wherever I go. I praise you, Father, that the Holy Spirit is the Spirit of truth that the world cannot take into its heart, because it doesn't recognize him. But you have given him to me to live forever in my heart. I bless you, Father!

October 11

When the Comforter is come, whom I will send unto you from the Father, even the Spirit of truth, which proceedeth from the Father, he shall testify of me (John 15:26).

Thank you, Father, that the Holy Spirit testifies to me of Jesus. I praise you that the Holy Spirit is the Spirit of truth, who rightly divides that which is not true from that which is true. I praise you that I can always depend on the Holy Spirit to reveal the truth to me in all situations in the world and also in your Word. I praise you, Father, that the Holy Spirit comes from you and not from the devil. I praise you, Jesus, that the Holy Spirit is constantly reminding me at all times of you and your love for me, of your sacrifice, and of your cleansing power. I thank you that he is also the Counselor, Helper, Advocate, Intercessor, and Strengthener.

October 12

And it shall come to pass afterward, that I will pour out my spirit upon all flesh; and your sons and your daughters shall prophesy, your old men shall dream dreams, your young men shall see visions (Joel 2:28).

Father, I'm going to stand right under the center of that spout. I praise you that you are pouring out your Spirit upon all flesh. I praise you that this includes me, and I thank you for pouring it all over me. Thank you that you are giving some of us the ability to dream dreams and others to have visions and prophesy. I thank you and praise you, Father, because your Spirit is blessing me more than ever before. I praise you that you didn't restrict the gift of the Holy Spirit to the Pentecostals, but that you have given it to the Baptists, the Methodists, the Catholics, the Presbyterians, the Episcopalians, and to whosoever will!

October 13

Therefore, brethren, we are debtors, not to the flesh, to live after the flesh. For if ye live after the flesh, ye shall die: but if ye through the Spirit do mortify the deeds of the body, ye shall live (Romans 8:12, 13).

I don't owe my flesh anything. Glory! Father, I thank you that I am not a debtor to the flesh, and therefore I don't have to live after the lust of the flesh, because you have plainly told me that if I do, I shall die. I thank you and praise you, Father, that through the power of the Spirit I am constantly putting to death the evil deeds prompted by the flesh, so that I may live. I thank you that it gets easier every day for me to turn from my carnal nature, because, through the power of the Holy Spirit constantly and habitually with me, I am putting to death the evil deeds prompted by my body.

October 14

But the fruit of the Spirit is love, joy, peace, longsuffering, gentleness, goodness, faith, meekness, temperance: against such there is no law (Galatians 5:22, 23).

I rejoice and praise you, Father, for the love in my heart. Thank you that the fruit of the Spirit, or the work his presence within me accomplishes, includes giving me the kind of love I never had before. Thank you that I can now love the unlovely. I thank you that I am running over with joy and peace and longsuffering. I praise you for gentleness, goodness, and faith. I praise you for meekness and self-control. I love you for giving me not just one of the fruits of the Spirit, but *all* of them. Thank you that I am a big bowl of spiritual fruit salad!

October 15

For as many as are led by the Spirit of God, they are the sons of God. For ye have not received the spirit of bondage again to fear; but ye have received the Spirit of adoption, whereby we cry, Abba, Father (Romans 8:14, 15).

I am a child of God! Father, I love you for leading me by your Spirit and for making me your child. I praise you for your Word, which assures me that I won't be left out, because you say *as many as are led*, and not just a select few, are the children of God. Thank you that I'm not caught up in slavery to fear, Father, but instead I've been adopted into your very own family. I rejoice and thank you for the presence and power of your Holy Spirit, who enables me to do the greater things your Word promises.

October 16

But this precious treasure—this light and power that now shine within us—is held in a perishable container, that is, in our weak bodies. Everyone can see that the glorious power within must be from God and is not our own (II Corinthians 4:7 LB).

I praise and thank you, Father, for the light inside my physical body that is right this minute shining out of me upon the world. I thank you for the divine light of the Gospel that shines so brightly that everyone knows it couldn't be from my own power but can only be *your* power shining and glowing through me. I praise you, Father, for making me a million-watt floodlight that shows the lost ones how to find you. I rejoice because the whole world can see that the grandeur and exceeding greatness of power and glory are yours.

October 17

Christ is not weak in his dealings with you, but is a mighty power within you. His weak, human body died on the cross, but now he lives by the mighty power of God. We, too, are weak in our bodies, as he was, but now we live and are strong, as he is, and have all of God's power to use in dealing with you (II Corinthians 13:3, 4 LB).

All of God's power is mine. Heavenly Father, how I praise you and worship you that Jesus is a mighty power within me. I thank you that his human body, though weak, died on a cross, that he was resurrected, and that he now lives by the mighty power of your Spirit. I thank you that, even though we are weak in our bodies, we have all your power to use to make our lives victorious at all times. Thank you, Father, for this divine privilege.

October 18

Yet to us God has unveiled and revealed them by and through His Spirit, for the (Holy) Spirit searches diligently, exploring and examining everything, even sounding the profound and bottomless things of God—the divine counsels and things hidden and beyond man's scrutiny (I Corinthians 2:10 Amp.).

Father, I thank you that you have revealed the secrets of the universe to us by and through your Holy Spirit. I praise you that the Spirit searches everything completely, thoroughly, effectually, wholly, and in every respect, and because I love you and obey you, you have made all the things that are beyond man's scrutiny and investigation available to me. I praise you, Father, that, because I have the mind of Christ, these truths are available to me.

October 19

But the natural man receiveth not the things of the Spirit of God: for they are foolishness unto him: neither can he know them, because they are spiritually discerned. But he that is spiritual judgeth all things, yet he himself is judged of no man (I Corinthians 2:14, 15).

I rejoice because I am not a natural (or unspiritual) person, Father. Because I'm not natural, I can receive *all* the wonderful things from the Spirit, which are nothing but foolishness and trivia to the natural person who cannot accept or welcome the wonderful gifts and teachings of the Holy Spirit. But you let me investigate and appraise all things, because I am a spiritual being. I praise you that, even though I judge all things and situations, I am judged of no one.

October 20

What is it then? I will pray with the spirit, and I will pray with the understanding also: I will sing with the spirit, and I will sing with the understanding also (I Corinthians 14:15).

I praise you, Father, that you give us two "hot lines to heaven." I thank you that I can pray and praise you with my mind and understanding, and I can also pray and praise you with my spirit through the power of the Holy Spirit. Sometimes there are feelings in my heart that just can't be expressed with the understanding, because they are so overwhelming. I thank you, Father, for giving me a special way to pray or praise you with my spirit to express these wonderful feelings. I thank you that I don't have to confine my singing to my understanding, but that my spirit can sing also!

October 21

For he that speaketh in an unknown tongue speaketh not unto men, but unto God; for no man understandeth him; howbeit in the spirit he speaketh mysteries (I Corinthians 14:2).

Thank you, Father, that you have given me an unknown tongue with which to praise you. I praise you that this special language is a private, personal, distinctive, and unique communication that I have with you. Men can't understand it, but you can, Father. I praise you that in the Spirit I can utter to you secret and hidden things that I don't understand, but your Spirit understands and answers my spirit. Thank you, Father, for the mysteries that my spirit converses with you about, which I have no way of understanding or knowing about, so that you can answer my prayers even before I utter them with my own understanding.

October 22

And the spirits of the prophets are subject to the prophets (I Corinthians 14:32).

Father, I praise you that you give us control over our own spirit. I thank you that when I speak in tongues I can stop and start at will, because the Holy Spirit is gentle and never forces me to do anything I don't want to do. I thank you, Father, that you have stored in my human body the power of the Holy Spirit, so that I can pray in tongues any time I want, and I can stop praying in tongues any time I want. I love you for this, Father. Thank you for the glorious privilege of singing in tongues whenever I want and stopping whenever I want.

October 23

And he that keepeth his commandments dwelleth in him, and he in him. And hereby we know that he abideth in us, by the Spirit which he hath given us (I John 3:24).

I thank you and praise you, glorious Father, for we know that you abide in us because of the Spirit you have given to us. Thank you, Father, that I don't have to wonder and question whether or not I belong to you, because your very own Spirit within me testifies to me that you dwell in me. Thank you for this positive proof that I am your child. I bless you, Father, for telling us that you dwell, reside, live, stay, and abide in us, which means you accept and endure us. Glory to you, Father, for such a great promise.

October 24

And the Spirit and the bride say, Come. And let him that heareth say, Come. And let him that is athirst come. And whosoever will, let him take the water of life freely (Revelation 22:17).

Father, I thank you and praise you that you said whosoever will may come and take of the water of life freely. Thank you that I am drinking at the fountain of living water. Thank you that your Spirit called me, and thank you that you are not stingy with the flow of that fountain, but you said that I can just drink and drink and drink. Father, I am a glutton for that living water, and I love you for giving from a bountiful supply. My heart is overflowing with gratitude and joy because of the wonderful things you say in your Word. I praise you that my soul is constantly refreshed, supported, and strengthened by it.

October 25

And when they bring you unto the synagogues, and unto magistrates, and powers, take ye no thought how or what thing ye shall answer, or what ye shall say: For the Holy Ghost shall teach you in the same hour what ye ought to say (Luke 12:11, 12).

How I praise and thank you, Father, that when I am in situations where I find it difficult to speak what is on my heart and I don't know the answers, your Holy Spirit teaches me quickly and wisely exactly what I need to say. I thank you that I don't have to be anxious or worried, but that I can always depend on your beautiful Holy Spirit to teach me the right words to say under all conditions.

October 26

There hath no temptation taken you but such as is common to man: but God is faithful, who will not suffer you to be tempted above that ye are able; but will with the temptation also make a way to escape, that ye may be able to bear it (I Corinthians 10:13).

Father, how I bless you for your Word. I'm so blessed because no enticement to sin, no matter where it comes from or where it leads to, will overcome me beyond human resistance because of your compassionate nature and understanding. I praise you because I can trust you to always provide the way out, so that I can be capable and strong and powerful to patiently bear up under whatever temptation comes my way. Father, because of your faithfulness to me, I shall be faithful to you, depending on your Word to keep me from falling on the slippery paths and ditches that lie alongside the straight and narrow path.

October 27

And my speech and my preaching was not with enticing words of man's wisdom, but in demonstration of the Spirit and of power: That your faith should not stand in the wisdom of men, but in the power of God (I Corinthians 2:4, 5).

Dear Father, I praise you that we don't have to be gifted orators with words that the world can't understand, but we simply have to be ordinary people who use your boldness to go out and share the gospel, which you back up with the power of your Holy Spirit. I thank you that I don't have to worry about what I say or to whom I say it, because your power will cause people to have faith in you and not in me. I love you, Father, for using me even though I'm nothing special, except in your Kingdom. Glory!

October 28

. . . *When the enemy shall come in like a flood, the Spirit of the Lord shall lift up a standard against him* (Isaiah 59:19).

Father, how I praise you that when the enemy roars around like a lion, or comes pouring into my life like a flood, I don't have to worry one tiny little bit, because your Spirit raises up a standard against him and puts him to flight. Father, I love you beyond measure, because I don't have to be afraid of the devil. I know at all times that your Spirit, in lifting up that standard, drives off the enemy. Thank you, Lord, that I'm always on the winning side. Thank you that I don't have to worry whether it's a trickle or a flood; your Spirit is always there to raise the right-sized standard. Thank you that I have victory!

October 29

. . . Not by might, nor by power, but by my spirit, saith the Lord of Hosts (Zechariah 4:6).

Heavenly Father, I praise you that I don't have to be a superhuman being who is full of strength, or a powerful individual who can shake mountains, because my battles are all won in the Spirit. I thank you, Father, that the same promise you gave to Zerubbabel applies to me—that all things are accomplished not by might, nor by power, but by your Spirit. I rejoice, Father, because your Spirit dwells in me. I thank you, Father, that the Holy Spirit is an endless source of oil and is not controlled by the countries or nations of the world, but by you. Hallelujah!

October 30

It is the spirit that quickeneth; the flesh profiteth nothing: the words that I speak unto you, they are spirit, and they are life (John 6:63).

How I praise you, Father, that it is the Holy Spirit who quickens my mind to understand the truths of your Word and statements made to me. I thank you, Father, that your words are Spirit and life. I thank you that, because of your Holy Spirit, your Word is alive and living in me today. I thank you that I don't have to be dead in sin the way I was, but that I now have life in the Spirit. I know that my flesh conveys no benefit whatever, and there is no heavenly profit in it. Your life-giving Spirit has made me come alive in Christ. I worship and praise you for this, Father!

October 31

And these signs shall follow them that believe; In my name shall they cast out devils; they shall speak with new tongues; They shall take up serpents; and if they drink any deadly thing, it shall not hurt them; they shall lay hands on the sick, and they shall recover (Mark 16:17, 18).

I'm a believer! Father, how I praise you, because you have promised that through your Holy Spirit, signs follow me because I believe. I thank you that I can use the name of Jesus and cast out devils and speak with new tongues. I thank you that serpents can't harm me, and if I accidentally drink something poisonous, your Spirit will protect me. I thank you and praise you, Father, that because of the power of your Holy Spirit, sick people recover when I lay hands on them. Hallelujah! Thank you for the signs that follow me wherever I go!

November

PRAISE AND THANKSGIVING

We celebrate Thanksgiving in the month of November. Thanksgiving is a time of great joy to all of us, as we settle back and remember *all* the things we need to thank God for on the special day that we set aside to praise him for our bountiful way of life.

Let's make *every day* in November a time of "thanks"giving!

We thank God for Jesus, the rock of our salvation. *The Lord is my rock, and my fortress, and my deliverer* (II Samuel 22:2).

We thank God for salvation through the blood of Jesus Christ. *In whom we have redemption through his blood. . .* (Ephesians 1:7).

We thank God for our marriage. *What therefore God hath joined together, let not man put asunder* (Matthew 19:6).

We thank God for our children. *As arrows are in the hand of a mighty man; so are children of the youth* (Psalm 127:4).

We thank God for supplying all of our needs according to his riches in glory by Christ Jesus! (See Philippians 4:19.)

We thank God for our grandchildren. *Children's children are the crown of old men. . .* (Proverbs 17:6).

We thank God for our ministry. *And he gave some, apostles; and some, prophets; and some, evangelists; and some, pastors and teachers; For the perfecting of the saints, for the work of the ministry, for the edifying of the body of Christ* (Ephesians 4:11, 12).

We thank God for his Word. *Heaven and earth shall pass away; but my words shall not pass away* (Mark 13:31).

We thank God for faith. . . . *God hath dealt to every man the measure of faith* (Romans 12:3).

Let's confess these praise and thanksgiving devotions at least ten times each day, so that our spirits will be soaring in the heavens every day this month.

November 1

I will bless the Lord at all times: his praise shall continually be in my mouth (Psalm 34:1).

Father, we bless you, we bless you, we bless you. All day long I bless you because of your goodness to me. I bless you because you are the magnificent Creator, who put the stars in the sky and separated the land from the sea. I bless you because you always keep your promises to us, even when fulfilling them requires miracles. I bless you, Father, because you have lifted me out of darkness and led me to victory. I bless you and praise you, for your praises are sweeter than honeycomb in my mouth. I praise you for your faithfulness to me. I praise you, Father, because it blesses me to keep your praises continually on my lips.

November 2

Be glad in the Lord, and rejoice, ye righteous: and shout for joy, all ye that are upright in heart (Psalm 32:11).

Glory, Father, I'm filled to overflowing with gladness in you. I'm glad because my whole life is in your hands. I can't stop rejoicing, because you have made me righteous through your glorious righteousness. You have made me upright, because your strength never fails. I can't keep silent, because if I did the very rocks would cry out. But I don't want to keep silent, for my heart tells me to shout for joy. Father, I have to sing and shout for joy, because you've not only given me a wonderful day today, but you've given me a wonderful future to look forward to in this life and the next. You've given me a wonderful forever.

November 3

Let my mouth be filled with thy praise and with thy honour all the day (Psalm 71:8).

My mouth declares your praises, Father, because in all ways you are worthy of my praise. I honor and rejoice in your name. Father, I really want to thank you that my mouth doesn't have to be filled with mockery and scorn, with contempt and complaints, with deceit and accusation—the filth of the world. I'm so filled with joy in praising you and your goodness that the world's conversation habits don't interest me in the slightest. I praise and honor you, because in all the blessings you bring to me and to my family—love, joy, peace, health, and prosperity—the glory belongs to you, Father. I honor you because you are a righteous and loving God, the Fountainhead of all blessings.

November 4

It is a good thing to give thanks unto the Lord, and to sing praises unto thy name, O most High! (Psalm 92:1).

Heavenly Father, I rejoice and give thanks to you; because you fill my life with so many good things, I overflow with feelings of thankfulness. I praise you, Father, and I thoroughly enjoy the abundance of blessings you bring to me because of who you are. How can I not be thankful for each bite of food when I love the Provider with all my heart? It is good to give thanks to you and sing your praises, because it pleases you and because it lifts up our hearts to you. By thanking you, I send you my love. By singing your praises, I send you my love. Thank you for the joy you put in my heart even from thanking you.

November 5

Make a joyful noise unto the Lord, all ye lands. Serve the Lord with gladness: come before his presence with singing. Know ye that the Lord he is God: it is he that hath made us, and not we ourselves; we are his people, and the sheep of his pasture. Enter into his gates with thanksgiving, and into his courts with praise: be thankful unto him, and bless his name (Psalm 100:1-4).

Father, I'm making a joyful noise, because I only want to talk about you and to celebrate your presence in my life with praise and thanksgiving. I serve you gladly with all my heart, mind, body, and soul, and I can't stand in your presence without singing, because you have made me so glad to be your child. I praise you that we can enter your gates with thanksgiving, and I thank you that we can enter your courts with praise. I bless and praise you, heavenly Father.

November 6

I will praise thee, O Lord my God, with all my heart; and I will glorify thy name for evermore (Psalm 86:12).

I praise you, Father, with all my heart and all my very being. I thank and praise you, because you made provision for forgiveness of my sins, you saved me from a life of eternal damnation through the sacrifice of your beloved Son, and you rescued me out of the miry clay to set my feet on solid rock. Glory, Father, I'm blessed to sing your praises, because there is so much for which to praise you. I love you and praise you with every fiber of my being, and I will glorify and lift up your holy name forever.

November 7

I will sing unto the Lord as long as I live: I will sing praise to my God while I have my being (Psalm 104:33).

Father, I thank you for the privilege of singing to you as long as I live. Singing to you is special to me, Father, because each song is an expression of thankfulness that reaches deep inside me to present an offering of joy beyond words. When I praise you in song, I feel as though you are touching me, as though you are lifting me up to you on the wings of that song. Heavenly Father, I thank you for listening to my songs; they always make me feel especially close to you. As long as there is breath left in my body, I will sing praises to you!

November 8

Let the heavens be glad, and let the earth rejoice: and let men say among the nations, The Lord reigneth (I Chronicles 16:31).

Glory, Father, the heavens are glad, the earth rejoices, and I'm saying over and over, *the Lord reigns, the Lord reigns, the Lord reigns!* Thank you, Father, for the way my spirit leaps within me when I say these wonderful words—*the Lord reigns*. I praise you for even putting into my heart and mouth these words that make my soul sing: *the Lord reigns*. You are the Creator and the Lord of all creation; I rejoice with the earth and join in heaven's gladness, because you are my Lord and you rule over my life as well as everything else—visible and invisible. Father, I'm overwhelmed with thankfulness, because, even though you have so much to care for, you take wonderful care of me!

November 9

By him therefore let us offer the sacrifice of praise to God continually, that is, the fruit of our lips giving thanks to his name (Hebrews 13:15).

Father, I offer the sacrifice of praise to you continually, even though it's no sacrifice to praise you, but a wonderful privilege. It gives me joy to praise you continually, because you bless me continually. You even bless me by the lift you give me while I'm praising you. Father, the fruit of my lips is always good fruit, especially in giving thanks to your name and in praising you for just being who you are. Let the fruit of my lips send out the fruit of your Spirit: love, joy, peace, longsuffering, gentleness, goodness, faith, meekness, and temperance. Father, you are the God of glory, and I love to praise you!

November 10

Then I will praise God with my singing! My thanks will be his praise—that will please him more than sacrificing a bullock or an ox. The humble shall see their God at work for them. No wonder they will be so glad! All who seek for God shall live in joy. For Jehovah hears the cries of his needy ones, and does not look the other way. Praise him, all heaven and earth! Praise him, all the seas and everything in them! (Psalm 69:30-34 LB).

I praise you, Father, while I'm singing. I thank you for all the good things in life. I praise you and thank you for my family, my health, my life, and, most important of all, my salvation. Father, I join my voice with all the things in heaven and earth and praise you. My voice is not as loud or strong as the sea, but I praise you with all my might!

November 11

Let everyone bless God and sing his praises, for he holds our lives in his hands. And he holds our feet to the path (Psalm 66:8, 9 LB).

Heavenly Father, we bless you and we sing, sing, sing your praises. Just as you hold all creation in your hands, you hold our lives right in the hollow of your hands. I bless and thank you for this, because in your hands we have everything—breath, life, and our very being. I bless you, Father, for saving, guiding, teaching, and nourishing me. You've given me not just life, but all the trimmings with it. It's a wonderful life, because you constantly show me how you want me to live and what you want me to do. You light the path in front of me, you hold my feet on that path, and you guard me from stumbling. Father, I bless you for this!

November 12

From the rising of the sun unto the going down of the same the Lord's name is to be praised (Psalm 113:3).

It's early in the morning, Father, and I'm praising you before I even get out of bed. I praise you because I have a warm bed to sleep in and a roof over my head. I praise you because the sun rises each day on your beautiful creation, and because the bright flowers, grass, and lofty trees testify to your glory. I praise you for the sunshine, for the rain, for the seasons, and for the food you put in my mouth. I praise you for all the wonderful things you give me to do each day and for opportunities to tell people about you. My lips are going to praise you this whole day—until the sun goes down, and then, Lord, I'm going to keep praising your name. Hallelujah!

November 13

. . . Believe in the Lord your God, so shall ye be established: believe his prophets, so shall ye prosper. And when he had consulted with the people, he appointed singers unto the Lord, and that should praise the beauty of holiness, as they went out before the army, and to say, Praise the Lord; for his mercy endureth for ever. And when they began to sing and to praise, the Lord set ambushments against the children of Ammon, Moab, and Mount Seir, which were come against Judah; and they were smitten (II Chronicles 20:20-22).

Father, I praise you that I am established and am prospering. I praise you for the fantastic power that there is in praise. Thank you, Father, that when the enemies came after your children, the very moment your children began to sing and praise, you caused the other armies to begin fighting among themselves, and they were destroyed. Thank you that, because I am your child, I'm on the winning side at all times. Hallelujah!

November 14

For I will pour water upon him that is thirsty, and floods upon the dry ground: I will pour my spirit upon thy seed, and my blessing upon thine offspring (Isaiah 44:3).

Pour it on me, Lord, because I'm thirsty. I praise you that you don't give me a tiny little straw to sip water when I'm thirsty, but you pour it all over me. I thank you that there is so much that it even pours off of me and floods the dry ground. Thank you that there is not only enough for me, but also for my offspring. I thank you that my children and their children are splashing in the overflow that you've given to me. I will bless you at all times, and your praise shall continually be in my mouth!

November 15

And when the trumpeters and singers were in unison, making one sound to be heard in praising and thanking the Lord, and when they lifted up their voice with the trumpets and cymbals and other instruments for song, and praised the Lord, saying, For he is good, for His mercy and lovingkindness endure for ever, then the house of the Lord was filled with a cloud, So that the priests could not stand to minister because of the cloud; for the glory of the Lord filled the house of God (II Chronicles 5:13, 14 Amp.).

Your glory surrounds praise. I praise you because the minute we begin to praise and bless you, your glory fills the temple to such an extent that at times we can't even stand on our feet. Bless you, Father, that you don't reserve all the good things for heaven, but you even let us have some of your glory down here. Bless you for power and majesty and glory so strong that I can't even stand up!

November 16

. . . Your love and kindness are better to me than life itself. How I praise you! I will bless you as long as I live, lifting up my hands to you in prayer. At last I shall be fully satisfied; I will praise you with great joy (Psalm 63:3, 4 LB).

Father, I search for you, and my soul thirsts for you. I rejoice in you, my God, because through the night you protect me in the shadow of your wings. My protection and success come from you alone. No enemy can reach me because of your love and kindness. Thank you for leading me to the mighty, towering rock of safety. I shall forever live in your tabernacle in the shelter of your wings. Thank you for all the blessings you reserve for those who call on your name.

November 17

O give thanks unto the Lord; call upon his name: make known his deeds among the people. Sing unto him, sing psalms unto him: talk ye of all his wondrous works. Glory ye in his holy name: let the heart of them rejoice that seek the Lord. Seek the Lord, and his strength: seek his face evermore. Remember his marvellous works that he hath done; his wonders, and the judgments of his mouth (Psalm 105:1-5).

Father, I sing praises to you. I talk of all your deeds and devoutly and earnestly make them known. Father, my heart rejoices, because I seek you as my indispensable necessity. I thank you that you are always there. Father, I shall seek your face all the days of my life and will remember all the wonderful and exciting deeds you have done. Hallelujah!

November 18

O come, let us sing unto the Lord: let us make a joyful noise to the rock of our salvation. Let us come before his presence with thanksgiving, and make a joyful noise unto him with psalms. For the Lord is a great God, and a great King above all gods (Psalm 95:1-3).

We praise you, glorious Father, and sing songs before you and make a joyful noise to you, because you are the rock of our salvation. Our hearts just want to glorify you. I make joyful noises to you, Father, with thanksgiving in my heart, and I enter before your presence with thanksgiving and songs of praise. You do so much for me that I just want to rejoice and celebrate before you. Father, I praise and thank you, because you are a great God and a great King above all gods, and you are *my God*.

November 19

Teach me thy way, O Lord; I will walk in thy truth: unite my heart to fear thy name. I will praise thee, O Lord my God, with all my heart: and I will glorify thy name for evermore. For great is thy mercy toward me: and thou hast delivered my soul from the lowest hell (Psalm 86:11-13).

Father, I praise you for teaching me your ways, so I can avoid the deceptions of the devil and walk in the truth. Tell me what to do, and I will do it. Tell me where you want me to go, and I will go there. Every fiber of my being unites in reverence and praise to your name. With every single bit of my heart I praise you and give glory to you, because you are so kind to me and have rescued me from deepest hell. Father, how could I help but praise you constantly?

November 20

Let the righteous be glad; let them rejoice before God: yea, let them exceedingly rejoice. Sing unto God, sing praises to his name: extol him that rideth upon the heavens by his name JAH, and rejoice before him (Psalm 68:3, 4).

Heavenly Father, I am uncompromisingly righteous because of your power, and I'm glad of it. My spirit is high, and I jubilantly rejoice, because I worship, follow, and obey the God of glory and righteousness. Father, just praising you makes my entire spirit and soul feel merry. My mouth is filled with your praise and your honor all day long, for you are the Lord of creation, the great God over the heavens. I sing your praises, because my tongue can't keep still in my mouth. I love you so much. Father, I rejoice before you—Jehovah is your name.

November 21

O clap your hands, all ye people; shout unto God with the voice of triumph. For the Lord most high is terrible; he is a great King over all the earth (Psalm 47:1, 2).

Father, we clap, clap, clap our hands and rejoice with all our hearts and all our minds as we shout triumphant praises to you. You are the Lord above all lords, the God above all gods, and you are awesome beyond words. The nations rise and fall at your command, and all the presidents, kings, premiers, and other world leaders have their power only because you allow it. Kings and kingdoms come and go, but your reign is forever, heavenly Father. I praise you because your power is exercised in righteousness and love toward all your people. Father, I thank you and praise you and shout praises to you at the top of my lungs because of *who you are.* Glory!

November 22

Oh, praise the Lord, for he has listened to my pleadings! He is my strength, my shield from every danger. I trusted in him, and he helped me. Joy rises in my heart until I burst out in songs of praise to him. The Lord protects his people and gives victory to his anointed king (Psalm 28:6-8 LB).

I bless you, Father, because you hear me whenever I cry out to you for help. I praise you because you are my entire strength in time of need, my impenetrable shield in time of danger. You are with me always, and I fear no evil, not even the devil himself. My heart just relaxes, my tensions disappear, because I trust, rely on, and confidently lean on you, and, Father, you never let me down. Because I am victorious in you, my heart is filled with joy, and I sing your praises. Glory!

November 23

I will declare thy name unto my brethren: in the midst of the congregation will I praise thee (Psalm 22:22).

I'll gladly praise you and talk about you to my relatives, Father, and you'll be there to soften their hearts and open their ears, because I can't handle some of that stubbornness of theirs without your help. Still, I'll praise you, because when they come to know you as I know you, Father, they'll want to praise you too! I will even stand up in front of the congregation, Father, and tell about all the wonderful things you have done. I will publicly state all my vows to you in the presence of those who love you and worship you, and I'll praise you in the midst of them. My heart rejoices with everlasting joy, and I worship you.

November 24

. . . *Then shall every man have praise of God* (I Corinthians 4:5).

Glory, Father, I praise you that on the very special day when we stand before you in judgment, you will examine us—even the most secret places of our hearts. Then the praise will be turned around and *you will give to us praise and commendation* for the things we have done on earth. Father, I always thought on that day I would have an opportunity to thank you in person for all the wonderful things you did for me down here on this earth. I thought I'd be able to thank you face to face for saving me, but your Word says you're going to thank *me!* I don't know how that can be, Lord, but I rejoice at the thought of that wonderful day to come. I'm going to do more for you than ever before, so I'll have lots of time to spend listening to you on that great day. That really turns me on, Father!

November 25

In God have I put my trust: I will not be afraid what man can do unto me. Thy vows are upon me, O God: I will render praises unto thee (Psalm 56:11, 12).

Father, I praise you and thank you, because my trust is entirely in you and not in my own strength, for with you as my fortress I'm not going to fear what any man can do to me. Criticism and ridicule can't harm me, for I am shielded by your truth. Enemies can't touch me, for you confound and confuse them, and they are defeated by your strength. I rejoice that your vows are upon me, Father, because in your strength and power and faithfulness, my victory is assured in all circumstances. Because I trust you with all my heart, you've made me a winner, Father, and I sing your praises!

November 26

Give unto the Lord, O ye mighty, give unto the Lord glory and strength. Give unto the Lord the glory due unto his name: worship the Lord in the beauty of holiness (Psalm 29:1, 2).

Thank you, Father, that I can come before you with praise, giving you the glory and strength you deserve for all you have done and are doing for your people. I glorify you, Father, for passing on to me the inheritance of Abraham. I glorify you for giving us your Word, so that we can find instruction and understanding. I glorify you for my salvation and the blessings that go with it. You are a mighty God, O Father, and you deserve all glory. I rejoice to worship you in the beauty of holiness.

November 27

Oh, sing out your praises to the God who lives in Jerusalem. Tell the world about his unforgettable deeds . . . He does not ignore the prayers of men in trouble when they call to him for help (Psalm 9:11, 12 LB).

I praise you, Father, and sing your praises around the world. My tongue just won't keep still, but breaks out in songs of praise, because you always hear us when we call to you, no matter what kind of trouble we are in. I praise you, Father, for your love and power, because your deeds in behalf of your people include many miracles, signs, and wonders. I will tell the world about them, so that your name is glorified among all the people of the earth. And how I bless you for not ignoring my prayers when I'm in trouble and yelling for help!

November 28

I will love thee, O Lord, my strength. The Lord is my rock, and my fortress, and my deliverer; my God, my strength, in whom I will trust; my buckler, and the horn of my salvation, and my high tower. I will call upon the Lord, who is worthy to be praised: so shall I be saved from mine enemies (Psalm 18:1-3).

How I love you, heavenly Father, because of all the tremendous things you have done for me. I praise you because you provide all that I need for my life. You are *my* rock, for I stand on the truth of your Word. You are *my* fortress, for I am safe in you. You are *my* strength, for I am victorious in you. You are *my* high tower, for I have wisdom in you. You are *my* deliverer, *my* salvation, and *my* God, for without you I would be lost in sin and darkness. I praise you, Father, for lifting me into your marvelous light!

November 29

Let them praise his name in the dance; let them sing praises unto him with the timbrel and harp (Psalm 149:3).

Father, I praise you with my dancing. I praise you for creating dancing as a form of worship to you, and just because the devil got into dancing doesn't mean I shouldn't worship you in the dance. I thank you for revealing the devil as a deceiver, who wants to hurt and limit righteous worship any way he can. Sometimes, Father, I get so filled with rejoicing in you and your music, I just have to clap my hands and move my feet. I sing your praises while I dance, and I'd play a tambourine or a harp if I could, just to praise you even more and glorify your name.

November 30

Praise him with the timbrel and dance; praise him with stringed instruments and organs. Praise him upon the loud cymbals: praise him upon the high sounding cymbals. Let everything that hath breath praise the Lord. Praise ye the Lord (Psalm 150:4-6).

I praise you, glorious Father, with everything I have that makes noise, because your Word tells me to make a joyful noise to you. Father, I clap my hands and sing and stamp my feet, just because I want to put everything I've got into worshipping and praising you. I can't play a timbrel, guitar, or organ, but I can bang two of my kitchen pan lids together to sound like cymbals! Father, because I have breath in me, I praise you, praise you, praise you. As long as I have breath, I'll continue to praise you. Thank you for another wonderful month!

December

SALVATION

As we wrote the devotions for December, they seemed to flow easier than any we've ever written.

Maybe it was because we've written them for twelve solid months.

Maybe it was because we felt a special anointing as we wrote them.

Maybe it was because we have a special love in our hearts for you.

Maybe it was because salvation is where it all starts. We pray as you confess them with us that your salvation will become more real and personal to you than it ever has been before. We know ourselves that, as we wrote these devotions, we once again became powerfully aware of the sacrifice of Jesus in our behalf.

December 1

But as many as received him, to them gave he power to become the sons of God, even to them that believe on his name (John 1:12).

Father, I received Jesus, and you received me. I praise you that, because I accepted Jesus as my Savior and Lord, you gave me the right, privilege, and power to become your child. Thank you that, because I believe on his name, I am restored to the fullness of your love, which is much greater than even the love we have for our own children. I thank you and praise you that the gates of heaven have been opened to me, because you sent your very own Son to call me to my eternal inheritance of everlasting life. I love you and worship you because you don't care what I used to be, you only see me for what I am today, *your child*. Hallelujah, Father, how I praise you for this wonderful blessing!

December 2

Except a man be born again, he cannot see the kingdom of God (John 3:3).

Thank you, Father, for sending your Son to tell us the wonderful way you have given us to see the Kingdom of heaven. I'm rejoicing because I've been born again of the Spirit, and I praise you for making the truth so simple for me. Father, I love you because you didn't set up some difficult and complicated test I had to pass to get into your Kingdom; you simply said I would have to be born again. I praise you that I don't have to guess or wonder about this, because you have given me the answer to eternal life in this one little sentence spoken by Jesus. Thank you, Father, for opening the windows of heaven to me. Thank you that, because I have been born again, I can and will see your Kingdom.

December 3

I am the way, the truth, and the life: no man cometh unto the Father, but by me (John 14:6).

I praise you, Father, that your Word makes the way to salvation and eternal life so clear and uncompromisingly direct. Jesus quite plainly said there was no other way to come to you except by him. I praise you, Father, that I'm not wasting time searching around for the way into heaven, because I've knocked on the door and Jesus opened it for me. Thank you, Father, for the truth your Son came to bring us and for the life I have because he lives in me. I rejoice that Jesus is *the* way, *the* truth, and *the* life. Thank you, Father. Thank you, Jesus.

December 4

For all have sinned, and come short of the glory of God (Romans 3:23).

Thank you, Father, that your Word tells me *all* have sinned and come short of the glory of God. You didn't leave any room for nit-picking about whether some are good enough to get into heaven the way they are. I praise you for making it clear that the law can't save us, that good words can't save us, that nothing we do on our own can save us because all have sinned, including me. Thank you, Father, that you have given me your Word, so that I might know what to do about my sins in order to be restored to you. I love you, Father. Thank you, Jesus, that all I did to be spiritually born was to confess that I had sinned, ask you to forgive my sins and come into my life, and I discovered I was born again!

December 5

For the wages of sin is death; but the gift of God is eternal life through Jesus Christ our Lord (Romans 6:23).

Heavenly Father, I praise and thank you for the most precious gift on earth—the gift of salvation. I thank you for showing me that the wages of sin in my life were death—death on this earth, because I didn't have your life flowing in me, and death to come in the torment of hell. Thank you, Father, for sending your wonderful Son, Jesus, to turn my life around. Thank you for snatching me out of the devil's hands and giving me a new life, filled to overflowing with your blessings. Thank you for the beautiful gift of eternal life in your glorious kingdom through Jesus. Glory!

December 6

For God so loved the world, that he gave his only begotten Son, that whosoever believeth in him should not perish, but have everlasting life (John 3:16).

I worship and praise you, Father, because you would have made the supreme sacrifice by sending your only Son to shed his blood on the cross *just for me*. Thank you, Father, for loving me so much that you were willing to let Jesus die, that I might have eternal life. I could never find it in my heart to let my son die for the world, but *you did*, and I can't thank you or praise you enough. I rejoice that I believe in your Son who gave his life that I might die to my sins and live in you, to your everlasting glory. I praise you, Father! I praise you, Jesus!

December 7

If we confess our sins, he is faithful and just to forgive us our sins, and to cleanse us from all unrighteousness (I John 1:9).

Father, how I love you for your faithfulness to me. We have all sinned, and because I have freely admitted and confessed my sins, I rejoice in the blessing of your forgiveness. Thank you, Father, that you have not only forgiven me, but you have cleansed me of all unrighteousness and buried my sins in the deepest sea, never to be remembered again. Hallelujah, Father, I'm clean! I'm walking in your light and your endless love, because I want to stay clean and because I love you with all my heart, soul, mind, and strength. Because you are faithful to me, I'm being faithful to you, and I'm blessed by the joy of life I have in you. Glory! How I rejoice that you always do what your Word says.

December 8

Behold, I stand at the door, and knock: if any man hear my voice, and open the door, I will come in to him, and will sup with him, and he with me (Revelation 3:20).

How I praise you, Jesus, for that day when you knocked on the door of my heart so loudly I had to open it and let you in. I thank you, Father, that Jesus said if I heard his voice he would come in to me and sup with me. *Because I heard him, he is living in my heart right now.* Thank you, Father, that I have the wonderful privilege of supping with Jesus, for I have never been so fully nourished in my whole life as I am now. I'm blessed because Jesus lives in me, I live in him, and the river of your living water is flowing through me. Thank you, Jesus, for the marvelous things that happened when I opened the door to *you!*

December 9

For he [God] hath made him [Christ] to be sin for us, who knew no sin; that we might be made the righteousness of God in him (II Corinthians 5:21).

Thank you, Father, that Jesus—the sinless, spotless, pure Lamb of God—was willing to take all the sin of the world upon his shoulders so that I might receive your righteousness in him. How I love you, Father, that you were willing to let your Son go through such a terrible ordeal for my sake. And how I love you, Jesus, because it didn't matter to you how horrible my sin was; you were willing to bear it on your innocent shoulders and take it to the cross for my salvation. Thank you, Father, thank you, Jesus, for loving me more than I can possibly know in this life. I rejoice and give thanks that, because I am dead to sin, I have everlasting life. Thank you for taking my sins and for filling me up with God's goodness in exchange. I received the best end of the bargain, and I love you for it!

December 10

That if thou shalt confess with thy mouth the Lord Jesus, and shalt believe in thine heart that God hath raised him from the dead, thou shalt be saved (Romans 10:9).

Father, I confess, I confess, I confess that *Jesus Christ is Lord!* I believe with all my heart, all my mind, all my strength, and all my soul that you raised him from the dead to show me the way to everlasting life. Because Jesus lives, I live. Father, these words bless my tongue and lips as I confess them, and I thank you and praise you for the love that fills my heart right this minute. Thank you, Father, that I am a new person in Jesus Christ; because I have believed, *I am saved!* Hallelujah!

December 11

For whosoever shall call upon the name of the Lord shall be saved (Romans 10:13).

Jesus, Jesus, Jesus. Heavenly Father, how I love to call upon the blessed name of Jesus, for I know that, because I have called upon the name of your Son, I am saved. Thank you that I am saved from darkness and called into your marvelous light, so that I might know the truth that is in Jesus Christ and be free at last. I praise you that now I have ears that hear your truth and eyes that see your truth, that Jesus is the way, the truth, and the life. I rejoice in the life you have given me. Thank you, Father, for choosing me to be in your Kingdom. I praise you that you are light, and there is no darkness in you at all!

December 12

For the Son of man is come to seek and to save that which was lost (Luke 19:10).

How I love you, Father, that I didn't have to worry and ponder about how to find Jesus and get his attention, because you love me so much that you sent him to find me. I was a lost sheep, and, even though Jesus had many sheep with him in his flock, I thank you that he came to rescue me personally. Jesus knew exactly where to look for me, because there was no way for me to escape the darkness and confusion of any sin on my own. Because I'm found and saved, I'm blessed in your love. Glory! I'm lifting up to you my loved ones who are not yet saved, and I thank you that Jesus hasn't stopped seeking and saving the lost. Because of your promises, I rejoice and am safe and secure in the knowledge that, as for me and my house, we will *all* be saved!

December 13

Therefore if any man be in Christ, he is a new creature: old things are passed away; behold, all things are become new (II Corinthians 5:17).

Father, how I bless you that I am grafted into Jesus Christ, that I am connected directly into him, locked in, fastened, attached, and joined to him exactly the same way a branch is connected to the vine, because I've been born again! I praise you that I am a brand-new person, because the life of Jesus pouring into my life has made me a fresh, new creation. Thank you, Father, that my old moral and spiritual condition is gone, gone, *gone*, washed away by the blood of the Lamb, because you love me so much. I praise you, Father, for giving me the blessing of new life!

December 14

For with the heart man believeth unto righteousness; and with the mouth confession is made unto salvation (Romans 10:10).

I believe, Father, with all my heart in your Son, Jesus, and I rejoice that, because Jesus lives in my heart, I am made righteous through him. Thank you, Father, that your righteousness is much, much more than the justice of this world. Your righteousness is perfect and without error, and because you are a wonderful, loving Father who cares for me, you have brought me into your perfect righteousness. Thank you, Father, for making salvation so simple in your Word, which says that if I believe in my heart and confess with my mouth, I am saved. I thank you and praise you for this big mouth of mine, Father, and I'm telling the whole world *I'm saved, I'm saved, I'm saved.* Hallelujah!

December 15

Who gave (yielded) Himself up (to atone) for our sins (and to save and sanctify us), in order to rescue and deliver us from this present wicked age and world order, in accordance with the will and purpose and plan of our God and Father (Galatians 1:4 Amp.).

Father, I praise and thank you that Jesus was willing to give up his life to save and sanctify me and to deliver me from the sin of this world. Father, as I look around at the sin and corruption so rampant in the world today, I rejoice and thank you for lifting me above all that carnal greed and desire, so that I can be about your business instead of the world's business. It really excites me to know that when you made out my individual plan, you put all the beautiful and wonderful things that you did in my life. I praise you for that!

December 16

And you hath he quickened, who were dead in trespasses and sins; Wherein in time past ye walked according to the course of this world, according to the prince of the power of the air, the spirit that now worketh in the children of disobedience (Ephesians 2:1, 2).

Father, how could you have ever loved me when I was dead in the graveyard of sin? I walked in those paths habitually, and yet you loved me enough to stop me from following the fashion of this world. I was under the temptations and pull of this present day when I was following the prince of the power of the air. I was under the control of the devil himself, but you grabbed me right out of the devil's hands and claimed me for your very own. How I praise you that, even though I was once rebellious and unbelieving and went against your purposes, you quickened my spirit. Father, I'll never be able to praise you enough!

December 17

Being justified freely by his grace through the redemption that is in Christ Jesus: Whom God hath set forth to be a propitiation through faith in his blood, to declare his righteousness for the remission of sins that are past, through the forbearance of God (Romans 3:24, 25).

Father, I fell so short of being an ideal person in your sight, and yet you declared me *not guilty.* I praise and thank you for your unmerited favor and mercy, which you freely and graciously gave to me. I thank you for the cleansing and life-giving sacrifice of the blood of your Son, Jesus, to save me from the stroke of your judgment. How I bless you for passing right over all the things I did and for ignoring them through forgiveness, in order to give me eternal life. I shall praise you forever and ever!

December 18

For we are his workmanship, created in Christ Jesus unto good works, which God hath before ordained that we should walk in them (Ephesians 2:10).

Father, I certainly wasn't any credit to you before I was saved, and I certainly didn't look like your handiwork. But how I praise you that I was created by you and born again in Jesus Christ! It really doesn't matter what I look like to the world, because I'm doing the job that you have always planned for me to do. Thank you, Father, that I am walking in your ways and living the good life according to the plan you had put into effect for me the moment I was born. Glory, Father, you've given me my own special path in life. It's mine, it's mine, it's mine, and no one else can walk it except me. Hallelujah!

December 19

And all of us, as with unveiled face, (because we) continued to behold (in the Word of God) as in a mirror the glory of the Lord, are constantly being transfigured into His very own image in ever increasing splendor and from one degree of glory to another; (for this comes) from the Lord (Who is) the Spirit (II Corinthians 3:18 Amp.).

Father, I praise you for the miracle you did in my life. I love you for transforming my life as I behold the glory of the Lord through your Word, transforming and transfiguring me ever more into your very own image in ways that I don't have to understand but simply accept. Father, I'm awed and thankful that you are changing me into ever increasing splendor and glory through the Spirit, and I rejoice at this mystery, because I am being prepared to meet you. Glory!

December 20

Neither is there salvation in any other; for there is none other name under heaven given among men, whereby we must be saved (Acts 4:12).

I rejoice in you, Father, for you understand everything, even though I don't. I don't understand computers; I don't understand rockets and space vehicles; I don't understand how television works. But I do understand and love the simplicity of your Word. How I praise you that I don't have to be a genius to know that there is salvation in no other name except the name of Jesus and to know that there is no other way I could have been saved except through that wonderful, majestic, powerful, and magnificent name of Jesus. Hallelujah!

December 21

Jesus said unto them, I am the bread of life: he that cometh to me shall never hunger; and he that believeth on me shall never thirst (John 6:35).

Heavenly Father, I love your bread. I praise you that I will never hunger again, because every day I feast spiritually on Jesus Christ—the bread of life. I praise and worship you because there can never be a thirsting in my soul; I'm drinking at that fountain of living water. Thank you for giving me true food and true drink, for in Jesus I am nourished to receive everlasting life and uplifted to live righteously in this world. Father, I love you for making such wonderful provisions for me.

December 22

And being made perfect, he became the author of eternal salvation unto all them that obey him (Hebrews 5:9).

I thank you and love you, Father, because Jesus is the author and source of eternal salvation for each and every one of us who gives heed to your Word and obeys you. I love you with all my heart, because, in spite of the pain you suffered in letting your only begotten Son bear the sins of the whole world in his human body on the cross, you did it because you loved me, just as Jesus did it because he loved me. Even if I'd been the only person in the world, Jesus would still have planned it this way. I love you, Father. I love you, Jesus.

December 23

In this was manifested the love of God toward us, because that God sent his only begotten Son into the world, that we might live through him. Herein is love, not that we loved

God, but that he loved us, and sent his Son to be the propitiation for our sins (I John 4:9, 10).

Father, in this world my mind can never understand the greatness of the love that prompted you to send your Son to be crucified, to die, and to be laid in a tomb until he should rise again, so that through him I might live—freed of the burdens of sin, redeemed in his blood, and restored to my inheritance of everlasting life in your heavenly Kingdom. How I praise you that it was not my love for you, but your love for me that made all this possible. When there was nothing I could do to be raised from death in my sins, you sent your Son to bring me back to life. Father, I bow down before you in adoration and praise.

December 24

Verily I say unto you, Except ye be converted, and become as little children, ye shall not enter into the kingdom of heaven (Matthew 18:3).

How I praise you, Father, and glorify your holy name, because you don't expect me to be a genius or intellectual giant to figure out salvation for myself. Instead your Son, Jesus, said I must come to you as a little child, with simple, uncomplicated faith. I love you, Father, for the teaching and instruction in your Word that let me understand exactly what I must do to enter into the Kingdom of heaven and abide in your glory. Thank you, Father!

December 25

For unto you is born this day in the city of David a Saviour, which is Christ the Lord. . . . And suddenly there was with the angel a multitude of the heavenly host praising God, and saying, Glory to God in the highest, and on earth peace, good will toward men (Luke 2:11, 13).

Father, today the world celebrates the birth of your Son. Saint and sinner alike, we celebrate this day. We praise you for that Good News, which came out of Bethlehem 2,000 years ago, and we praise you for the fact that the same Good News is going out all over the world today, touching hearts and quickening spirits just like it did long ago. Father, today I praise you for my salvation, and I pray for the world. May kings and nations feel your precious presence on this beautiful day of days!

December 26

Labour not for the meat which perisheth, but for that meat which endureth unto everlasting life, which the Son of man shall give unto you: for him hath God the Father sealed (John 6:27).

It's the day after Christmas. What a mess! Tinsel that's falling off the tree, wrapping paper torn apart in haste, broken ornaments, sorry toys, leftover turkey. Father, may we not look at the meat that perishes and the things that pass away, but may we work and seek after the lasting food that continues until eternal life. Yesterday I felt so spiritual, and today I'm so tired; but I praise you that you're just as real, just as special, just as magnificent, and just as trustworthy as you were yesterday. I bless you that as I clean up the mess, I can still give thanks and praise to you!

December 27

And they sung a new song, saying, Thou art worthy to take the book, and to open the seals thereof: for thou wast slain, and hast redeemed us to God by thy blood out of every kindred, and tongue, and people, and nation (Revelation 5:9).

Heavenly Father, I offer praise and gratitude for letting me peek into the last days through your Word. Thank you, Father, for letting me know, know, *know* that my Lord Jesus Christ is worthy to take the book of the seven seals and to open those seals, because he alone was slain and sacrificed. With his precious blood, he purchased people from every tribe and language and people and nation to serve you. You've made us a royal race of priests to our God, and we shall reign over the entire earth as kings. Father, how I praise you that you didn't leave me out of this wonderful world of your love.

December 28

Verily, verily, I say unto you, He that heareth my word, and believeth on him that sent me, hath everlasting life, and shall not come into condemnation; but is passed from death unto life (John 5:24).

My ears are open to your words, Father. I thank you for what Jesus said, and I hear it loud and clear. It makes my heart beat with joy to shout out, *I believe, I believe, I believe!* I bless you because I know that, since I believe and trust in you and cling to you and rely wholly on you, I now possess eternal life. Thank you that I do not come into judgment, will never incur a sentence of judgment, and will not come under condemnation, but that I have already passed out of death into life. I thank you that, because I believe in you through Jesus, I have the blessing of eternal, everlasting, continual, ceaseless, timeless, infinite, unending, immortal, imperishable, deathless life. Glory!

December 29

Jesus said unto her, I am the resurrection, and the life: he that believeth in me, though he were dead, yet shall he live: And whosoever liveth and believeth in me shall never die. Believest thou this? (John 11:25, 26).

I will never die. What a glorious thought! Jesus, you raise the dead and give them life again. I bless you that, even though this mortal body shall die, the real me shall live and never die. I thank you for that blessed hope. Father, I glorify you for sending Jesus to save me, and I will forever have faith in him, cleave to him, and rely on him until my very last mortal breath, when I shall take on immortality and breathe a different kind of breath. I believe, I believe, *I believe!*

December 30

Jesus said to her, Did I not tell you and promise you that if you would believe and rely on Me, you should see the glory of God? (John 11:40 Amp.).

I want to see your glory, Father. Jesus, I want to see your glory. I wait with excitement and anticipation for that greatest day when you've promised I shall see the glory. Thank you for equipping me and perfecting me toward that day, when I will at last stand before your throne and behold your glory and see you face to face. Father, how I long for that moment when I shall see your wonderful face. I don't even know what to expect glory to look like, but I'm excited thinking about what it will be like to walk into your presence in heaven for the first time. I'm stimulated and stirred up to see your glory and grace!

December 31

No man can come to me, except the Father which hath sent me draw him: and I will raise him up at the last day (John 6:44).

Father, I praise you for drawing me. As we celebrate the end of another year, I praise you that, even though this is the last day of this year, the most important day of all is that "last day" when all your children will all be raised up to spend eternity in heaven with you and Jesus! Father, I bless you for having blessed me all this year. I bless you and praise you for divine health. I bless you and praise you for your goodness, for your prosperity, for your loving-kindness. But most of all, I bless you for the assurance of my salvation!

If you have never asked Jesus into your heart, why don't you stop right now and say this simple little prayer:

> Father, I want eternal life. It is the desire of my heart, but I know that I have done things that are not pleasing to you. I have sinned, and I ask your forgiveness. Cleanse me of all unrighteousness. Jesus, I open the door to my heart and my life and invite you to come in. Take control of my entire life, and make me the kind of person you want me to be. Now I thank you, Jesus, for hearing my prayer and for coming into my heart as you promised. I love you, Jesus.

Now confess with your mouth these beautiful words: *I'm saved, I'm saved, I'm saved!*